Donna Kooler's
555 Timeless Cross-Stitch Patterns

Sterling Publishing Co., Inc. New York
A Sterling/Chapelle Book

Chapelle Ltd.

Owner: Jo Packham

Editor: Susan Jorgensen

Staff: Areta Bingham, Kass Burchett, Ray Cornia, Marilyn Goff, Karla Haberstich, Holly Hollingsworth, Barbara Milburn, Caroll Shreeve, Karmen Quinney, Cindy Stoeckl, Kim Taylor, Sara Toliver, Desirée Wybrow

Photography: Kevin Dilley/Hazen Photo Studio

Photo Stylist: Jill Dahlberg

Kooler Design Studio, Inc.

President: Donna Kooler

Vice President & Editor: Priscilla Timm

Executive Vice President: Linda Gillum

Staff Designers: Barbara Baatz, Linda Gillum, Nancy Rossi, Jorja Hernandez, Sandy Orton, Thomas Taneyhill, Pam Johnson

Design Assistants: Sara Angle, Jennifer Drake, Laurie Grant, Virginia Hanley-Rivett, Marsha Hinkson, Karen Million, Char Randolph,

Library of Congress Cataloging-in-Publication Data Available

If you have any questions or comments, please contact:

Chapelle, Ltd., Inc.,
P.O. Box 9252 Ogden, UT 84409
(801) 621-2777 •
FAX (801) 621-2788
e-mail: chapelle@ chapelleltd.com
website: www.chapelleltd.com

10 9 8 7 6 5 4 3 2 1

Published by Sterling Publishing Co., Inc.,
387 Park Avenue South, New York, NY 10016
© 2003 by Kooler Design Studio, Inc.
Distributed in Canada by Sterling Publishing
℅ Canadian Manda Group, One Atlantic Avenue, Suite 105
Toronto, Ontario, Canada M6K 3E7
Distributed in Great Britain and Europe by Chrysalis Books
64 Brewery Road, London N7 9NT, England
Distributed in Australia by Capricorn Link (Australia) Pty. Ltd.
P.O. Box 704, Windsor, NSW 2756, Australia
Printed in USA
All Rights Reserved

Sterling ISBN 0-8069-9357-X

Table of Contents

General Instructions
4

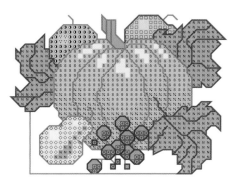

General Instructions

Introduction

Contained in this book are over 555 cross-stitch designs. Each double-page spread of graphed designs has its own color code. Each sampler's code is placed with the graphed sampler. To create one-of-a-kind motifs, vary colors in graphed designs.

Cross-stitch Items to Know

Fabric for Cross-stitch

Counted cross-stitch is worked on even-weave fabrics. These fabrics are manufactured specifically for counted-thread embroidery, and are woven with the same number of vertical as horizontal threads per inch.

Because the number of threads in the fabric is equal in each direction, each stitch will be the same size. The number of threads per inch in even-weave fabrics determines the size of a finished design.

Number of Strands

The number of strands used per stitch varies, depending on the fabric used. Generally, the rule to follow for cross-stitching is three strands on Aida 11, two strands on Aida 14, one or two strands on Aida 18 (depending on desired thickness of stitches), and one strand on Hardanger 22.

For backstitching, use one strand on all fabrics. When completing a French Knot (FK), use one strand and one wrap on all fabrics, unless otherwise directed.

Finished Design Size

To determine the size of the finished design, divide the stitch count by the number of threads per inch of fabric. When a design is stitched over two threads, divide stitch count by half the threads per inch. For example, if a design with a stitch count of 120 width and 250 height was stitched on a 28-count linen (over two threads making it 14 count), the finished size would be 8⅝" x 17⅞".

$$120 \div 14" = 8\tfrac{5}{8}" \text{ (width)}$$

$$250 \div 14" = 17\tfrac{7}{8}" \text{ (height)}$$

$$\text{Finished size} = 8\tfrac{5}{8}" \text{ x } 17\tfrac{7}{8}"$$

Preparing Fabric

Cut fabric at least 3" larger on all sides than the finished design size to ensure enough space for desired assembly. To prevent fraying, whipstitch or machine-zigzag along the raw edges or apply liquid fray preventive.

Needles for Cross-stitch

Blunt needles should slip easily through the fabric holes without piercing fabric threads. For fabric with 11 or fewer threads per inch, use a tapestry needle #24; for 14 threads per inch, use a tapestry needle #24, #26, or #28; for 18 or more threads per inch, use a tapestry needle #26 or #28. Avoid leaving the needle in the design area of the fabric. It may leave rust or a permanent impression on the fabric.

Floss

All numbers and color names on the codes represent the DMC brand of floss. Use 18" lengths of floss. For best coverage, separate the strands and dampen with a wet sponge, then put together the number of strands required for the fabric used.

Centering Design on Fabric

Fold the fabric in half horizontally, then vertically. Place a pin in the intersection to mark the center. Locate the center of the design on the graph. To help in centering the designs, dots are provided at the center top or bottom and center side. Begin stitching all designs at the center point of the graph and fabric. Black outlines extending from graphs indicate repeat of design.

Securing Floss

Insert needle up from the underside of the fabric at starting point. Hold 1" of thread behind the fabric and stitch over it, securing with the first few stitches. To finish thread, run under four or more stitches on the back of the design. Avoid knotting floss, unless working on clothing.

Another method of securing floss is the waste knot. Knot floss and insert needle down from the top left side of the fabric about 1" from design area. Work area. Cut off the knot and secure thread under worked stitches.

Carrying Floss

To carry floss, run floss under the previously worked stitches on the back. Do not carry thread across any fabric that is not or will not be stitched. Loose threads, especially dark ones, will show through the fabric.

Cleaning Finished Design

When stitching is finished, soak the fabric in cold water with a mild soap for five to ten minutes. Rinse well and roll in a towel to remove excess water. Do not wring. Place the piece face down on a dry towel and iron on a warm setting until the fabric is dry.

Stitching Techniques

Backstitch (BS)

1. Insert needle up between woven threads at A.

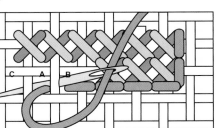

2. Go down at B, one opening to the right.

3. Come up at C.

4. Go down at A, one opening to the right.

Cross-stitch (XS)

Stitches are done in a row or, if necessary, one at a time in an area.

1. Insert needle up between woven threads at A.

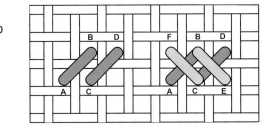

2. Go down at B, the opening diagonally across from A.

3. Come up at C and go down at D, etc.

4. To complete the top stitches creating an "X", come up at E and go down at B, come up at C and go down at F, etc. All top stitches should lie in the same direction.

French Knot (FK)

1. Insert needle up between woven threads at A, using one strand of embroidery floss.

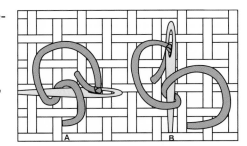

2. Loosely wrap floss once around needle.

3. Go down at B, the opening across from A. Pull floss taut as needle is pushed down through fabric.

4. Carry floss across back of work between knots.

Winter Wonders

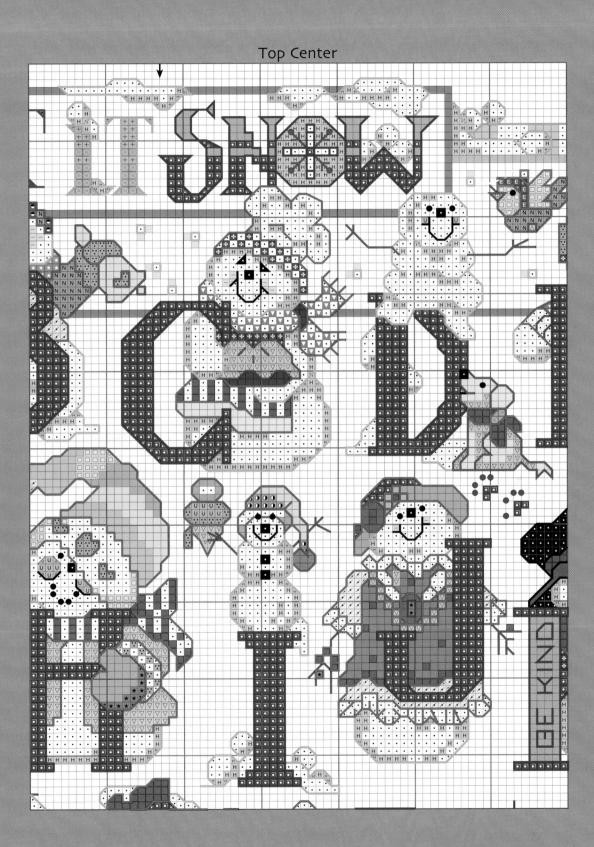

Top Right

DMC Floss			
	XS	BS	FK
White	·		
712			
3823			
744			
743	△		
5282	■		
722	◑		
353			
352	+		
351	◎		
349	■		
963	−		
3326	U		
899	⦂		
304	✚		
3608	■		
3607	E		
211			
210	▨		
208	■		●
3756			
775	H		
3755			
798	◪		●
747	▢		
598	▦		
959	N		
958	◧		
955			
913	★		
3817			
3816	▼		
561	■		
738	▽		
402			
3776	✦		
400	■		●
317	■		●
310	▣		●

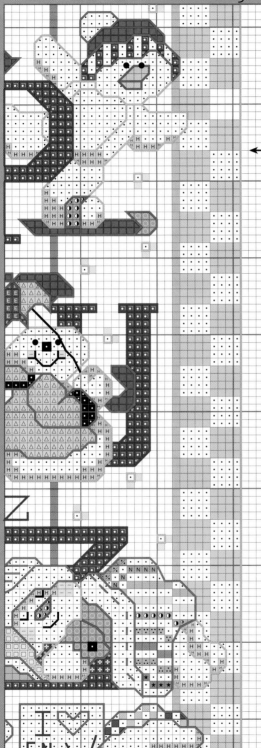

DMC Floss			
	XS	**BS**	**FK**
White	·		
712	▢		
3823	◩		
744	▢		
743	△	⌐	
5282	◼	⌐	
722	◐		
353	▢		
352	+		
351	◉	⌐	
349	◼	⌐	
963	−		
3326	U		
899	⦂	⌐	
304	✚	⌐	
3608	◼		
3607	E		
211	▢		
210	▨		
208	◼	⌐	●
3756	▢		
775	H		
3755	◼	⌐	
798	◙	⌐	●
747	▢		
598	⦂		
959	N		
958	◙	⌐	
955	▢		
913	★		
3817	▢		
3816	▽		
561	◼	⌐	
738	▽		
402	▢		
3776	⭐		
400	◼	⌐	●
317	◼		●
310	◼	⌐	●

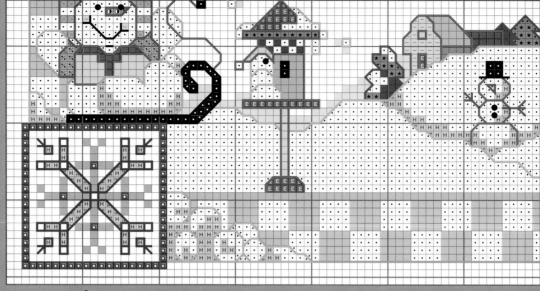

Bottom Left

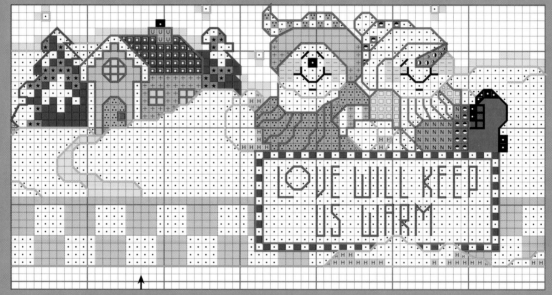

Bottom Center

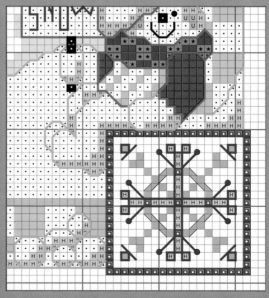

Bottom Right

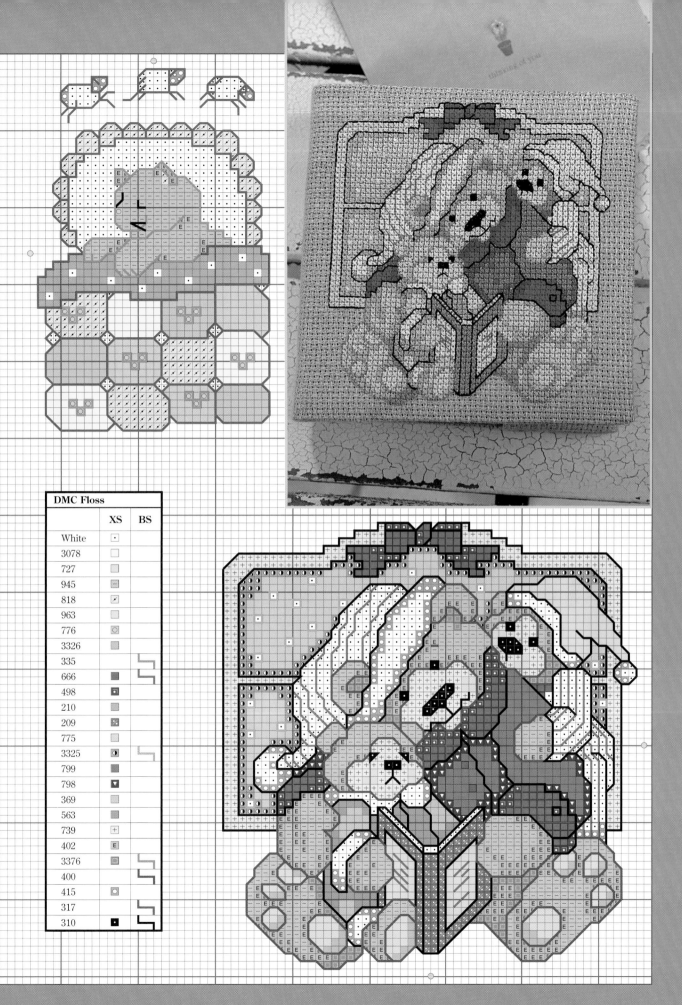

DMC Floss		
	XS	BS
White	·	
3078		
727		
945		
818		
963		
776	◎	
3326		
335		
666		
498		
210		
209		
775		
3325	◐	
799		
798	▼	
369		
563		
739	+	
402	E	
3376		
400		
415	◎	
317		
310	■	

DMC Floss			
	XS	BS	FK
White	·		
725	◪		
676	△		
744	U		
742	▢		
783	▨		
3708	⊠		○
963	▢		
3326	▢		
335	▢		
666	■		
498	▣		
3688	◎		
3687	■		
3685	✦	⌐	
210	▨		
208	■		
3837		⌐	●
775	▢		
827	H		
3325	◑		
799	■		
798	▼		
312		⌐	●
747	◇		
964	Z		
958		⌐	
704	K		
3347	■		
739	+		
738	▨		
434		⌐	
921	⊞		
762	▢		
415	◙	⌐	
318	■		
317		⌐	
310	▪	⌐	●

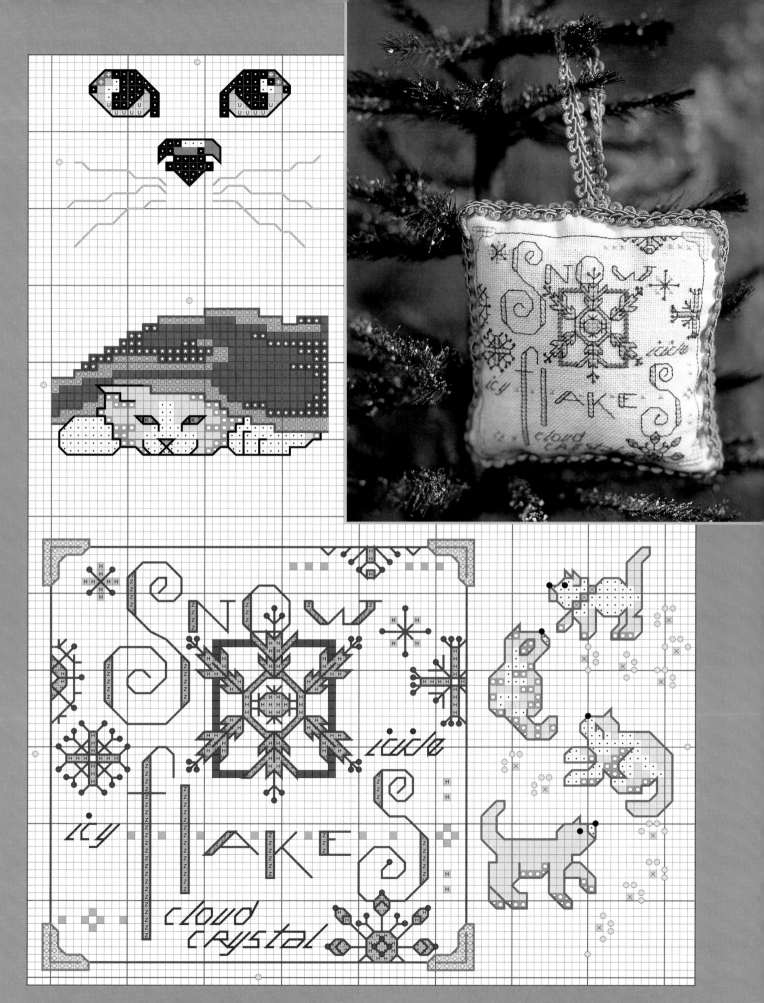

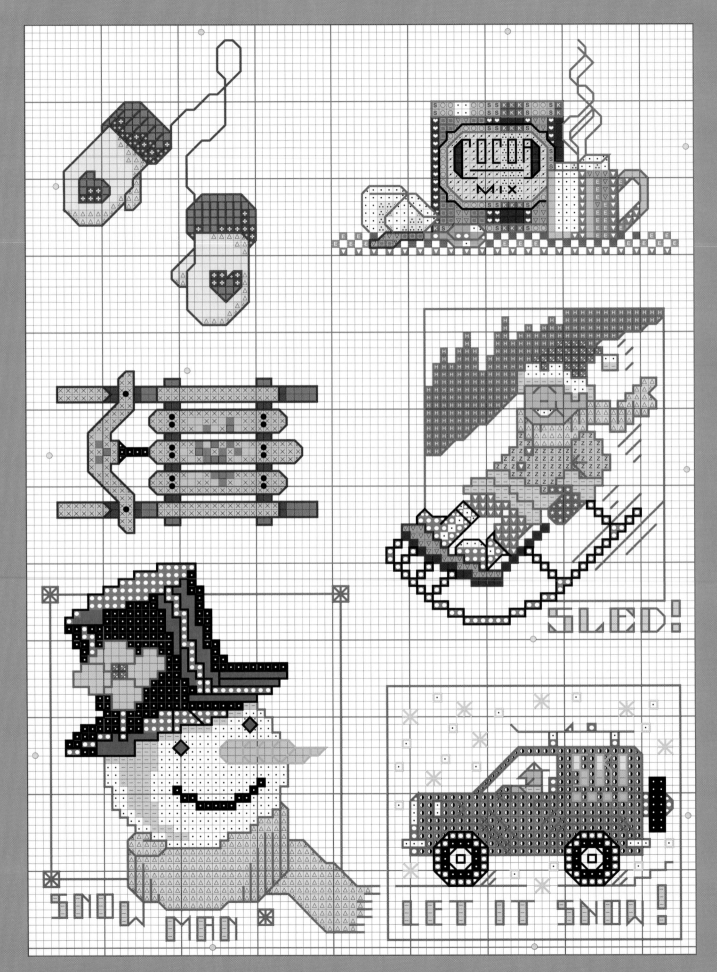

SLED!

SNOW MAN

LET IT SNOW!

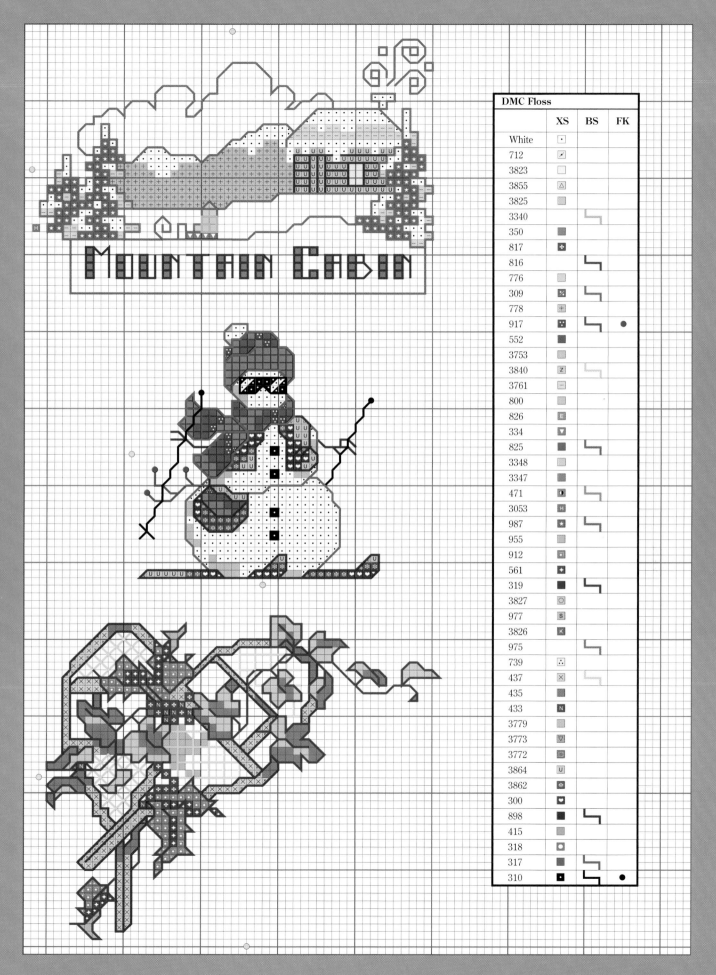

MOUNTAIN CABIN

DMC Floss			
	XS	BS	FK
White	·		
712	◪		
3823	☐		
3855	△		
3825	▨		
3340		⌐	
350	■		
817	✚		
816		⌐	
776	☐		
309	▨	⌐	
778	✚		
917	▨	⌐	●
552	■		
3753	▨		
3840	Z	⌐	
3761	−		
800	▨		
826	E		
334	▼		
825	■	⌐	
3348	☐		
3347	■		
471	◑	⌐	
3053	H		
987	✱	⌐	
955	▨		
912	▣		
561	✚		
319	■	⌐	
3827	◎		
977	S		
3826	K		
975		⌐	
739	⊡		
437	✕	⌐	
435	■		
433	N		
3779	▨		
3773	▽		
3772	▩		
3864	U		
3862	✱		
300	♥		
898	■	⌐	
415	▨		
318	▣		
317	■	⌐	
310	▣	⌐	●

19

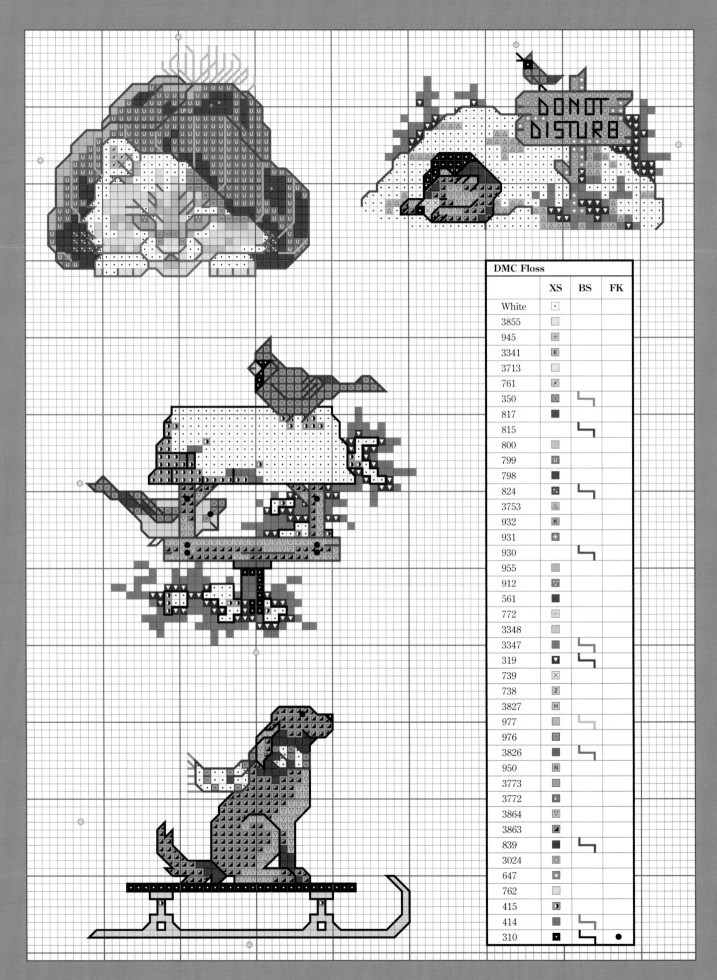

DMC Floss			
	XS	BS	FK
White	·		
3855			
945	+		
3341	E		
3713			
761			
350	◎	⌐	
817	◖		
815		⌐	
800			
799	U		
798			
824	⊠	⌐	
3753	△		
932	K		
931	✚		
930		⌐	
955			
912	⊡		
561			
772	−		
3348			
3347		⌐	
319	▼	⌐	
739	✕		
738	Z		
3827	H		
977		⌐	
976	▣		
3826		⌐	
950	N		
3773			
3772	⊡		
3864	▽		
3863	◪		
839		⌐	
3024	◎		
647	★		
762			
415	◑		
414		⌐	
310	▣	⌐	●

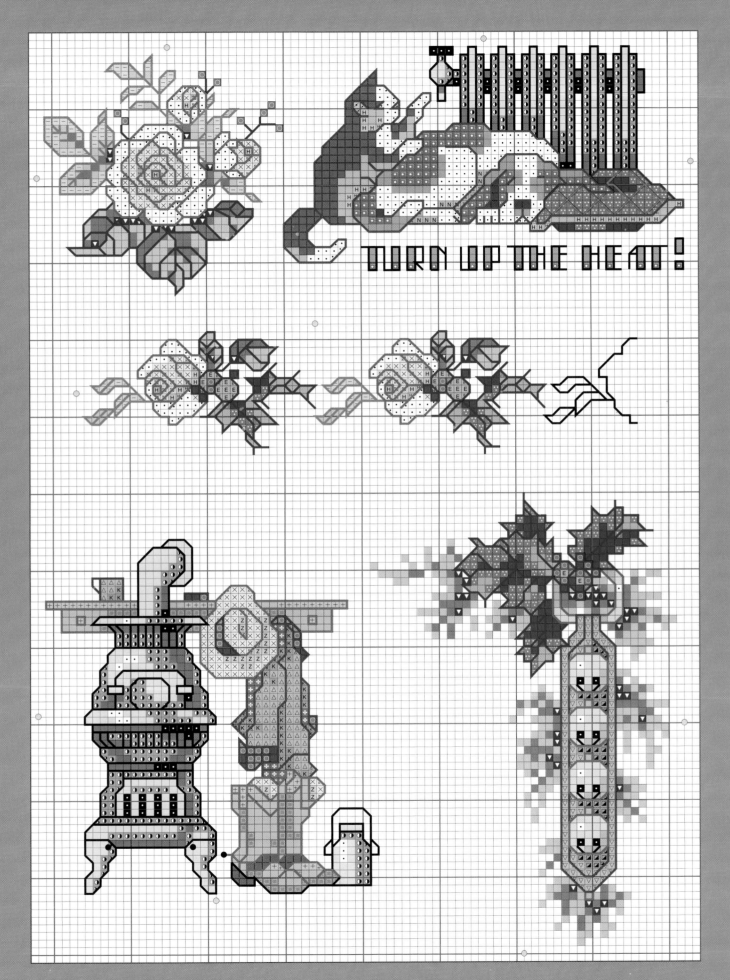

TURN UP THE HEAT!

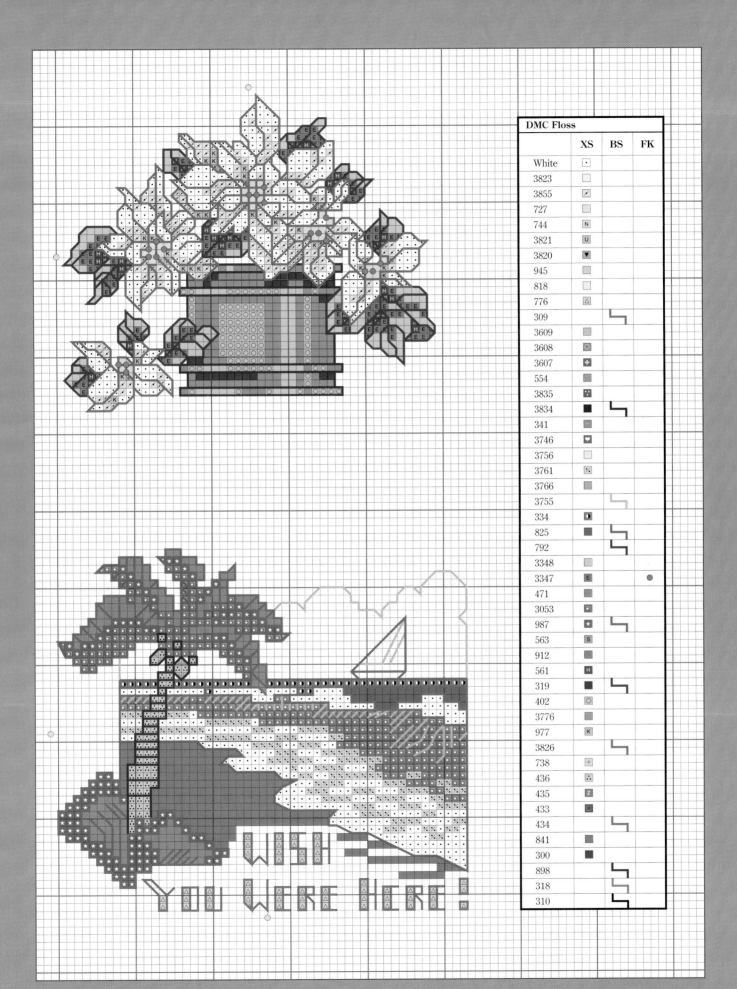

DMC Floss			
	XS	BS	FK
White	·		
3823			
3855			
727			
744	N		
3821	U		
3820	▼		
945			
818			
776	△		
309		⌐	
3609			
3608	◎		
3607	✛		
554			
3835	⊡		
3834	■	⌐	
341			
3746	♥		
3756			
3761	⅍		
3766			
3755		⌐	
334	◐		
825	■	⌐	
792		⌐	
3348			
3347	E		●
471			
3053	⊡		
987	⊡	⌐	
563	S		
912			
561	H		
319	■	⌐	
402	◎		
3776			
977	K	⌐	
3826		⌐	
738	+		
436	⁑		
435	Z		
433	▣		
434		⌐	
841			
300	■		
898		⌐	
318		⌐	
310		⌐	

DMC Floss			
	XS	**BS**	**FK**
White	·		
3823			
745			
744			
676			
729		⌐	
951			
754			
350		⌐	
666	◎	⌐	
304	✚		●
209	✕		
208	E		
3607			
3747			
3746	★		
775	⊞		
3325			
799		⌐	
322			
312		⌐	
959			
3812		⌐	
3813			
502	H		
703			
3012	△		
955	U		
912	✚		
988		⌐	
986		⌐	●
3827	Z		
436	▢	⌐	
434			
3774	S		
3773	K		
3772	▣		
3864			
3782	▽		
840	♥		
648			
646	◪		
415			
414			
844			
3799	△	⌐	●

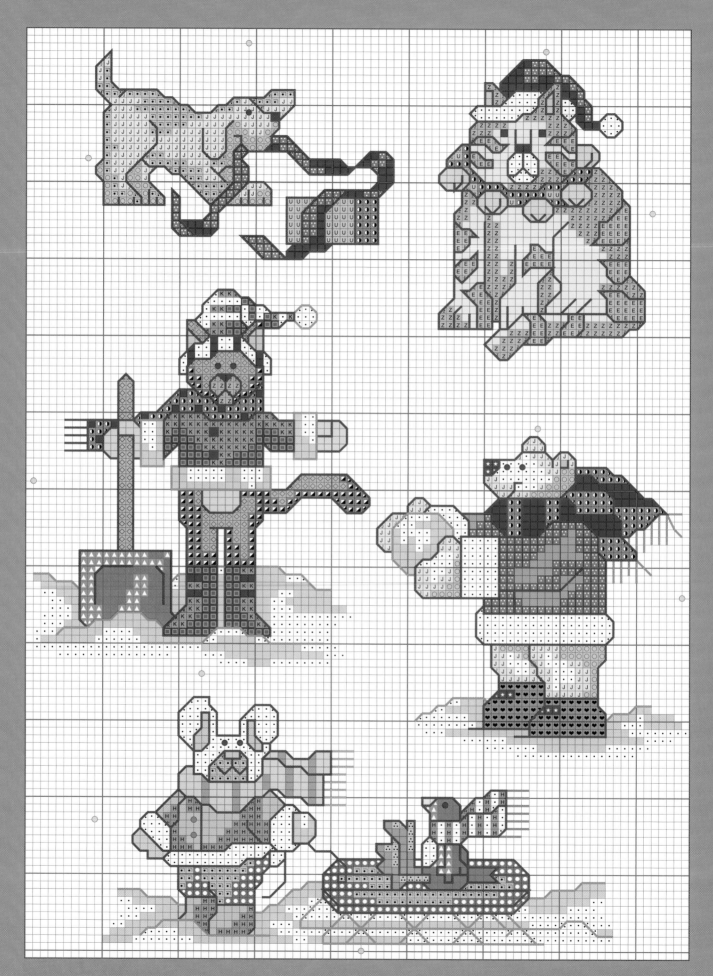

DMC Floss			
	XS	BS	FK
White	·		
3823			
745			
744			
677	−		
676	Z		
3820			
951	×		
945	+		
754			
722		⌐	
947	K		
350			
666			
304			
776			
3609			
3607		⌐	
211			
209			
3840	U		
775			
799		⌐	
798		⌐	
369			
954	H		
912		⌐	●
367		⌐	
3813	▽		
502			
3856			
3827	E		
402	◇		
3776			
739	J		
738	○		
437			
435			
434		⌐	
3773	△		
3064	♥		
3772			
3781			
3033			
648	▲		
646			
3799		⌐	●

27

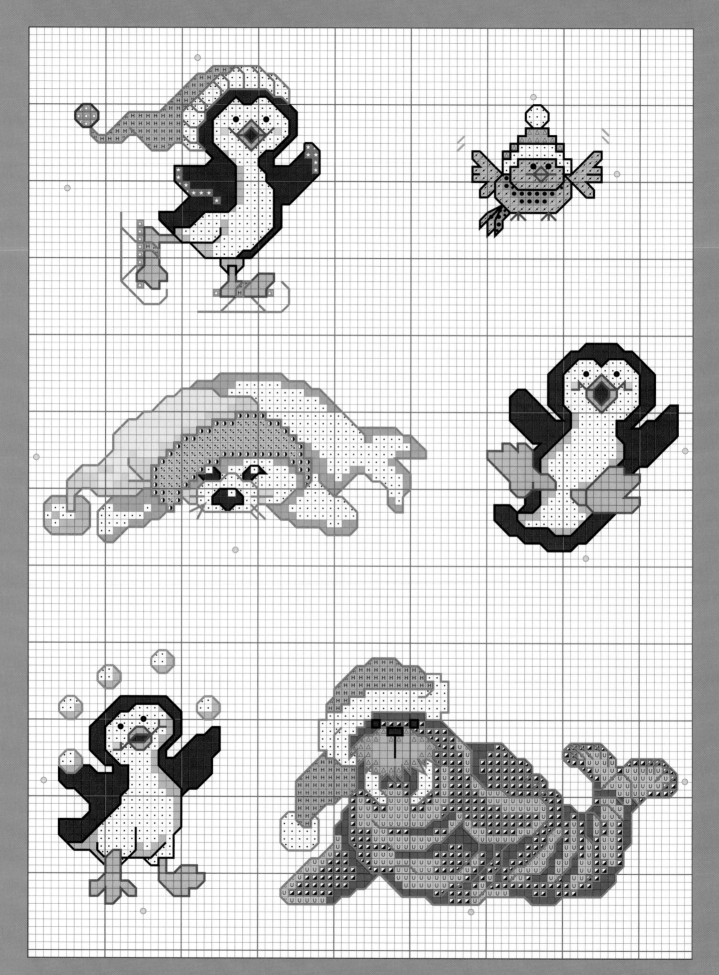

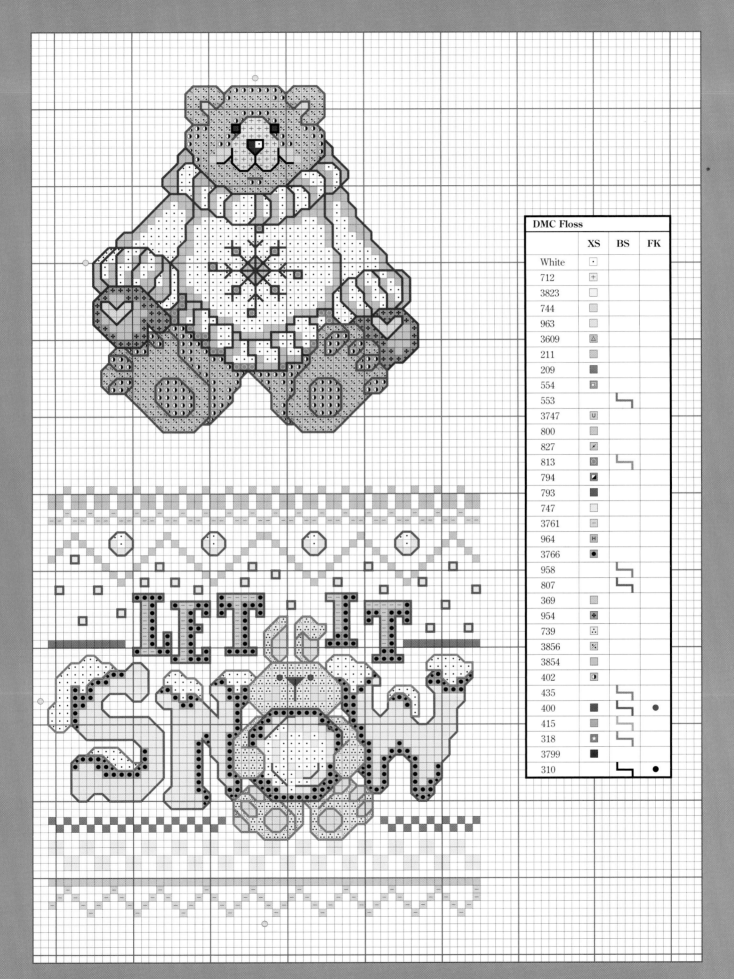

DMC Floss			
	XS	BS	FK
White	·		
712	+		
3823			
744			
963			
3609	△		
211			
209			
554	◘		
553		⌐	
3747	U		
800			
827	◪		
813	◉	⌐	
794	◪		
793			
747			
3761	−		
964	H		
3766	●		
958		⌐	
807		⌐	
369			
954	✦		
739	⋮		
3856	▨		
3854			
402	◑		
435		⌐	
400	■	⌐	●
415		⌐	
318	★	⌐	
3799	■		
310		⌐	●

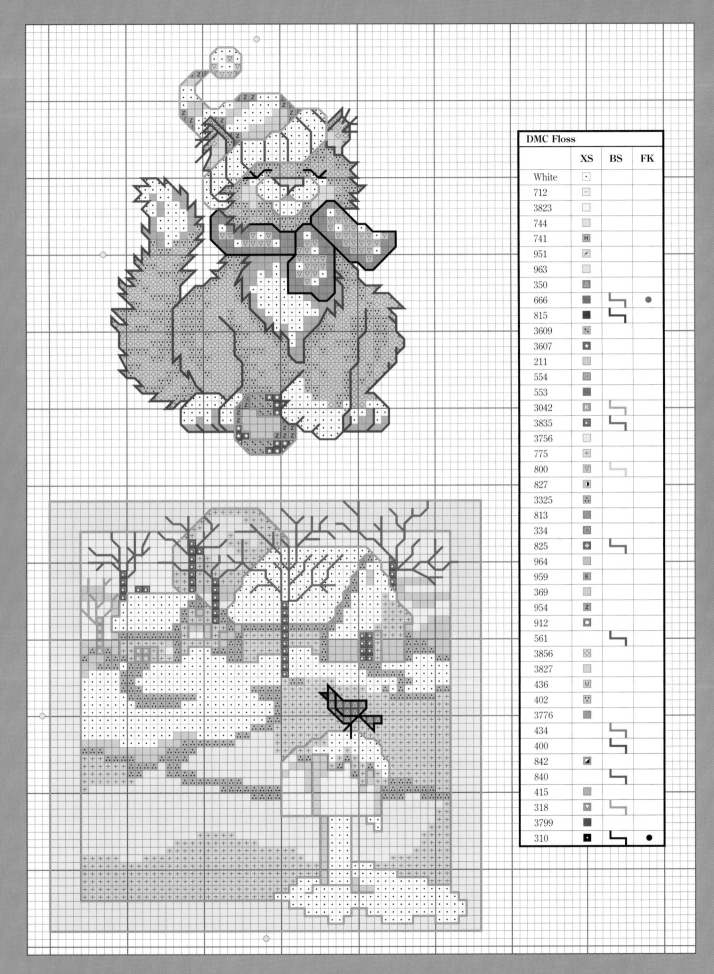

DMC Floss			
	XS	BS	FK
White	·		
712	−		
3823	☐		
744	☐		
741	H		
951	◪		
963	☐		
350	◹		
666	◼	⌐	●
815	◼	⌐	
3609	▨		
3607	★		
211	☐		
554	◎		
553	◼		
3042	K	⌐	
3835	▣		
3756	☐		
775	+		
800	▽	⌐	
827	◑		
3325	▨		
813	◼		
334	▣		
825	✛	⌐	
964	☐		
959	E		
369	☐		
954	Z		
912	◙		
561		⌐	
3856	◈		
3827	☐		
436	U		
402	▦		
3776	◼		
434		⌐	
400		⌐	
842	◪		
840		⌐	
415	☐		
318	▽	⌐	
3799	◼		
310	◼	⌐	●

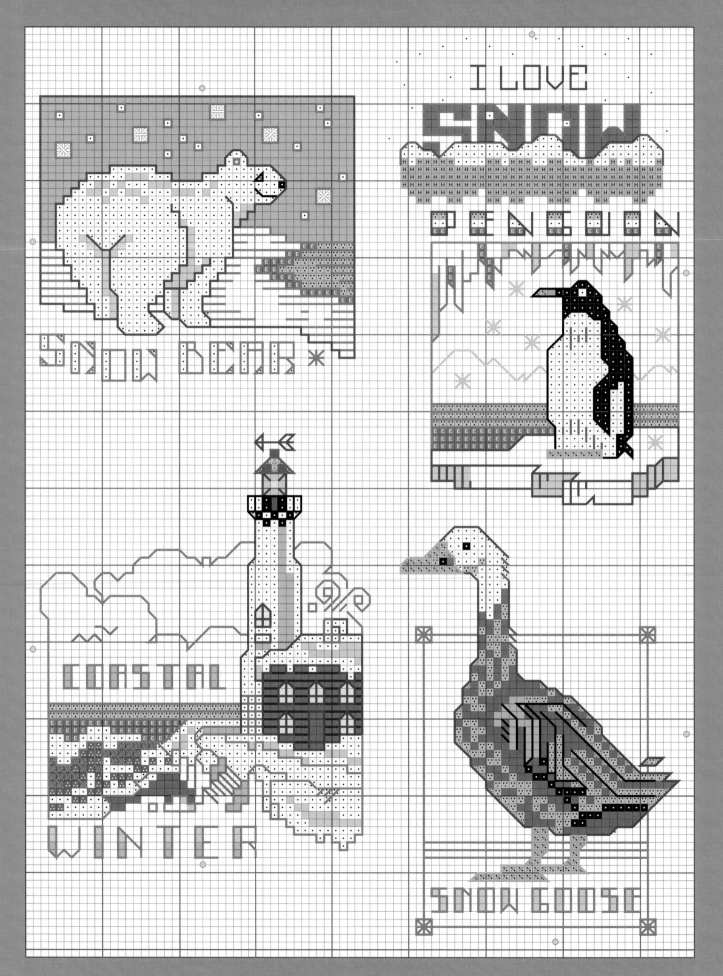

I LOVE SNOW

PENGUIN

SNOW BEAR

COASTAL

WINTER

SNOW GOOSE

DMC Floss			
	XS	BS	FK
White	·		
445			
780			
3825			
3340			
776	△		
778			●
309			
3753	H		
3761			
3840			
813			
799			
334	E		
824			
3053			
3347			
890	▼		
319			
3864	◎		
841			
3862			
839			
898			●
3024			
318	✶		
317			
310	▪		

Spring Fever

APRIL SHO

Top Right

DMC Floss			
	XS	**BS**	**FK**
White	⊡		
745	☐		
3855	⊞		
742	K		
741	☐		
720	◑		
352	☐		
351	H		
818	☐		
963	◢		
894	E		
309	■		
816	⊡		
3609	⬚		
3607	◉		
718	✚		
915	■	⌐	
210	☐		
553	△		
747	☐		
3761	✕		
813	■		
826	⊡	⌐	
824	★	⌐	
3813	☐		
3816	Z		
3348	☐		
989	■		
987	⊡		
986	■		
895	◘	⌐	
3827	▽		
3776	U		
301	■	⌐	●
400	◻		
919	♥		
543	☐		
3864	N		
3863	■		
762	☐		
318	▼		
317	■	⌐	●
310	■	⌐	

Middle Left

DMC Floss			
	XS	BS	FK
White	·		
745			
3855	+		
742	K		
741			
720	◖		
352			
351	H		
818			
963	✦		
894	E		
309			
816	⋮		
3609	▨		
3607	◎		
718	✚		
915		⌐	
210			
553	△		
747			
3761	✕		
813			
826	◉	⌐	
824	★	⌐	
3813	▢		
3816	Z		
3348			
989			
987	⋮		
986			
895	◘	⌐	
3827	▽		
3776	U		
301		⌐	●
400	▣		
919	♥		
543			
3864	N		
3863			
762			
318	▼		
317		⌐	●
310	▪	⌐	

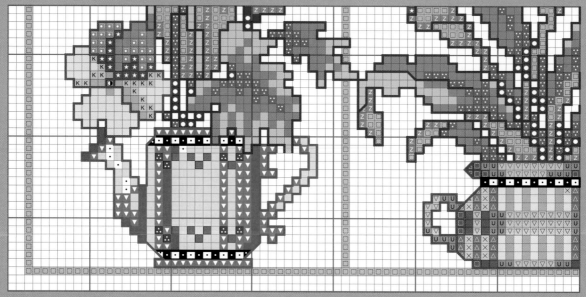

Bottom Left

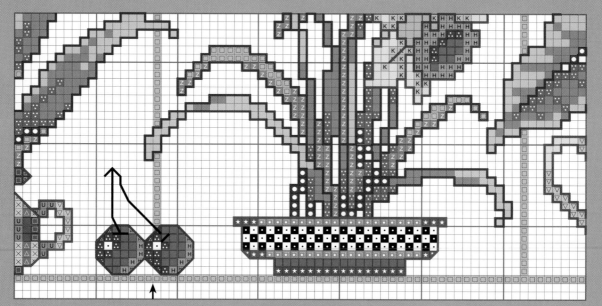

Bottom Center

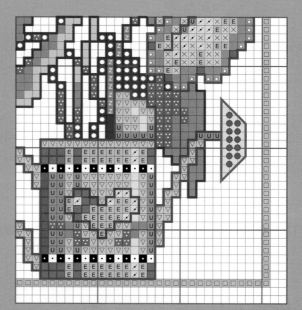

Bottom Right

42

DMC Floss			
	XS	BS	FK
White	·		
744	⊠		
722			
818			
963	−		
3326			
899	Z		
335	▣	⌐	
309	★	⌐	
775			
800	+		
3325	E		
813	⠂		
334			
562		⌐	
772	▽		
704			
702	▪		
699	■	⌐	
3864			
3863	✦		
437			
435	◨		
3826	◪		
975		⌐	
413		⌐	
310	▪		●

Friends
are the
in life's
garden

44

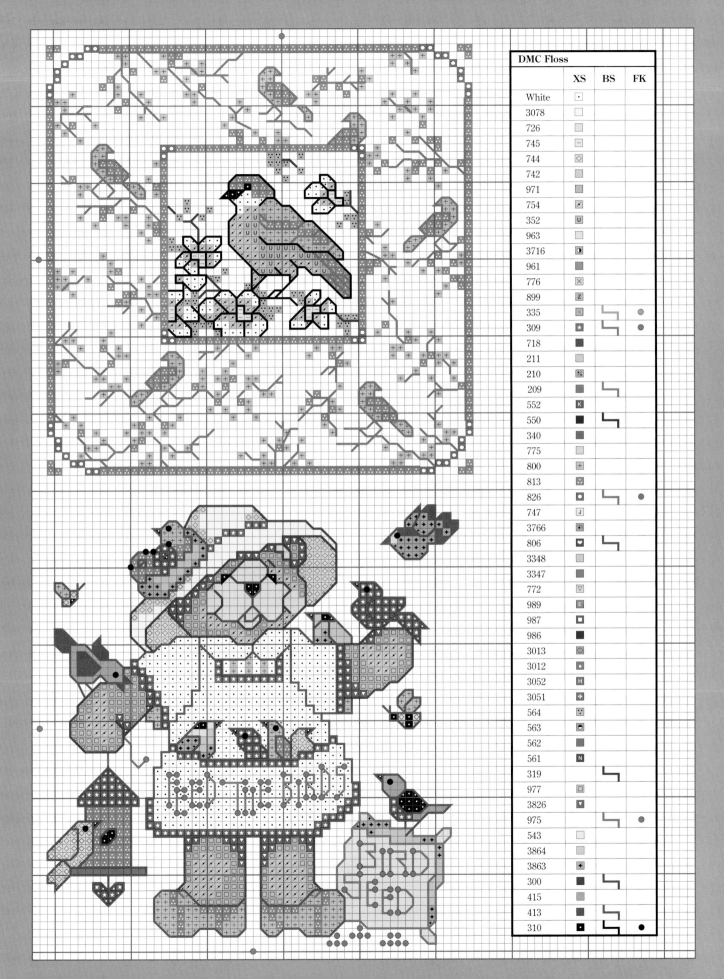

DMC Floss			
	XS	BS	FK
White	·		
3078			
726			
745	−		
744	◇		
742			
971			
754	∕		
352	U		
963			
3716	◑		
961			
776	✕		
899	Z		
335	▣	⌐	●
309	★	⌐	●
718			
211			
210	▨		
209		⌐	
552	K		
550		⌐	
340			
775			
800	⊞		
813			
826	◉	⌐	●
747	J		
3766	⊡		
806	♥	⌐	
3348			
3347			
772	▽		
989	E		
987	□		
986			
3013	◎		
3012	▲		
3052	H		
3051	✛		
564	⊡		
563	◓		
562			
561	N		
319		⌐	
977	▣		
3826	▼		
975		⌐	●
543			
3864			
3863	✦		
300		⌐	
415			
413		⌐	
310	▪	⌐	●

45

DMC Floss			
	XS	BS	FK
White	·		
745			
744	+		
743	◪		
742			
740			
722	K		
947	◕		
606	⊡		
963			
957	△		
3609	✂	⌐	
3608			
554	⊡		
209	✚		
208	N		
341	E		
340			
3746	★		
3753			
800	⊟	⌐	
813	U		
825	▼		
824		⌐	
3766			
807	⊡		
3817	Z		
3816	◪		
369			
954	✦		
912	◉		
563	H		
562			
561		⌐	
739	✕		
436		⌐	◉
402	⬚		
3776	▽		
920		⌐	●
3827	◎		
977	⊡		
3826		⌐	
762	J		
415			
414	▦		
413		⌐	●
310		⌐	

DMC Floss			
	XS	BS	FK
White	·		
745	◪		
727	▣		
725	◈		
972	▣	⌐	
741	U		
783	◑		
780		⌐	
948	▢		
758	＋		
3825	▣		
3340	N		
946	▣	⌐	
3713	─		
776	▣		
3706	E		
899	✚		
352	H		
351	◎		
350	▢		
326	▣	⌐	●
817	★	⌐	●
209	▣	⌐	
3761	▢		
775	Z		
3325	▣		
334	▣		
824		⌐	
704	▣		
703	▨		
700	♥		
699	■	⌐	
955	K		
913	◧		
988	▣	⌐	
3778	◙	⌐	
3830		⌐	
437	⊡		
436	◪		
434	▣	⌐	
801		⌐	
318		⌐	
3799	■	⌐	●
310	◼		

HUMMINGBIRD

PICNIC

Spring Showers

DMC Floss			
	XS	**BS**	**FK**
White	·		
3823			
727	−		
725		⌐	
676	Z		
741	⁞		
3825			
947			
818			
3716	N		
961	□		
3708	+		
3609	U		
603			
601	✛		
666	⁙		
817	■		
815	K	⌐	
211	◇		
210			
209	△		
208	◨		
554	◪		
333	★		
3834	■	⌐	
3747			
340	◉		
3746	⁙		
3813	✕		
502			
501	◐	⌐	
3817	△		
3816	E		
3364	H		
472	▽		
471			
772			
3346	▣		
319	■	⌐	
739	S		
437	▽		
3828	N	⌐	
829	■	⌐	●
402	J		
922	◪		
301	■	⌐	
801		⌐	
762			
318		⌐	
317	■		
413		⌐	●

Spring Bee Sprung

DMC Floss			
	XS	**BS**	**FK**
White	·		
712			
727			
725			
972	Z		
971			
783			
780			
721			
720			
900		⌐	
894			
893	U		
891			
309	E	⌐	
815			
814		⌐	
211			
210			
209			
208			
327		⌐	
827	×		
813		⌐	
825	H		
824		⌐	●
772			
3348	−		
3347			
3346			
3345			
3364			
3363			
3362			
890		⌐	●
913	N		
911		⌐	●
3825			
739			
738	S		
437			
436		⌐	
435	J	⌐	
920		⌐	
801		⌐	●
762			
415			
414			
318			
317		⌐	
413			
310		⌐	●

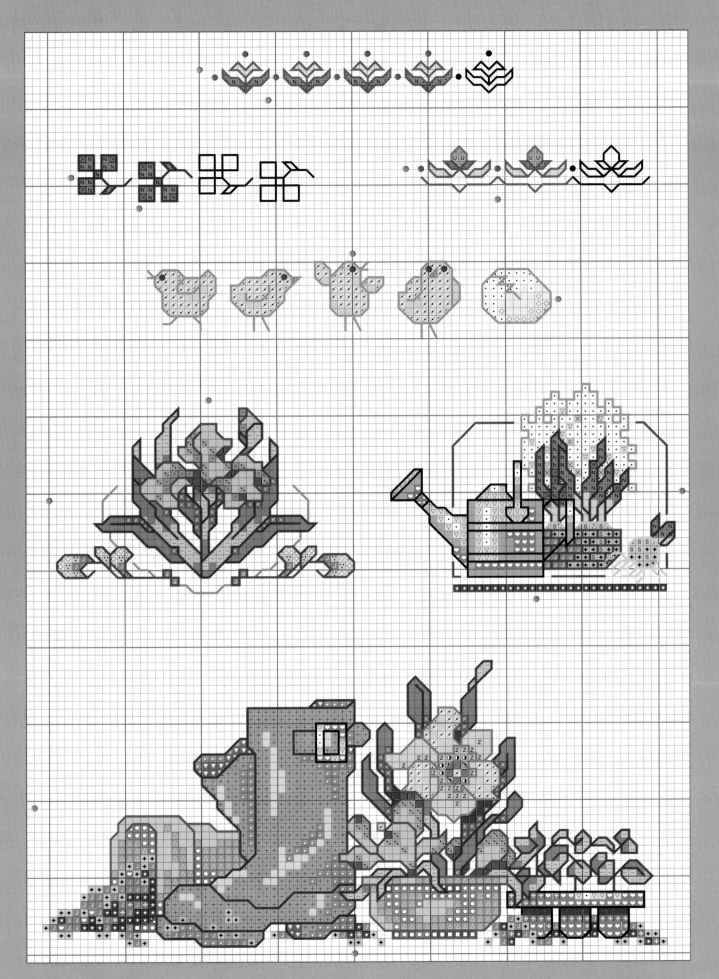

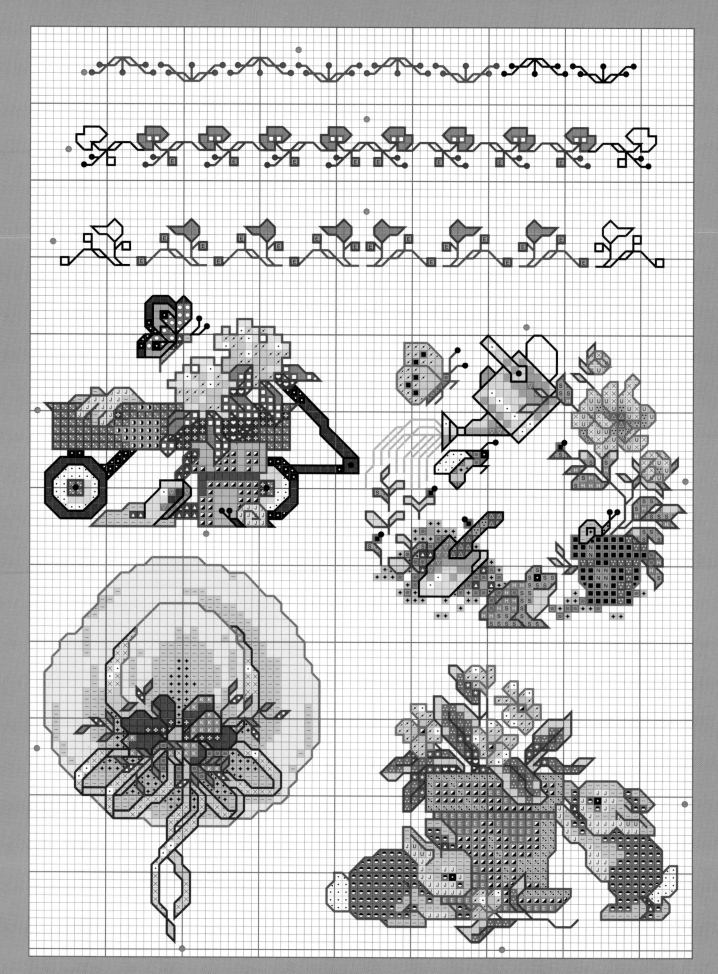

DMC Floss			
	XS	BS	FK
White	·		
3823			
727			
725			
3825			
722	N		
721	■		
900			
947	◐		
818	✕		
3708			
776	U		
899			
603	K		
601	■		
309	△	⌐	
606	■		
666			
817	Z		
815	✚	⌐	●
3834		⌐	
3325		—	
334	◓		
772			
704	▣		
727 472 }	◇		
472	E		
471	■		
3011	▣	⌐	
906			
904	★		
3348	+		
3347	▽		
3346	□		
3345	■		
3364	S		
3363	H		
3362	◎		
319	♥	⌐	●
739	J		
437	▭		
436	✦		
435	■		
434	▣	⌐	
402			
922	◪		
921	E		
301	■		
801	▲	⌐	●
762			
415			
318	▽		
413	■		
310	■	⌐	●

Southern Spring

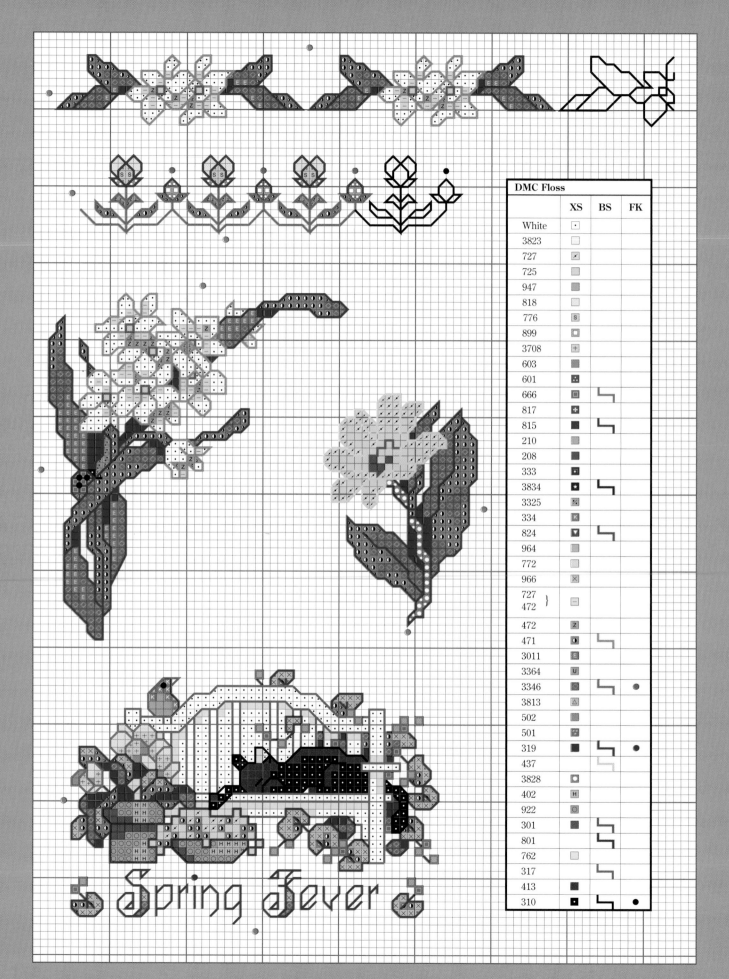

DMC Floss			
	XS	BS	FK
White	·		
3823			
727			
725			
947			
818			
776	S		
899			
3708	+		
603			
601			
666		⌐	
817			
815		⌐	
210			
208			
333			
3834		⌐	
3325			
334	K		
824		⌐	
964			
772			
966	X		
727 472	}	⌐	
472	Z		
471		⌐	
3011	E		
3364	U		
3346		⌐	●
3813	△		
502			
501			
319		⌐	●
437		⌐	
3828			
402	H		
922			
301		⌐	
801		⌐	
762			
317		⌐	
413			
310		⌐	●

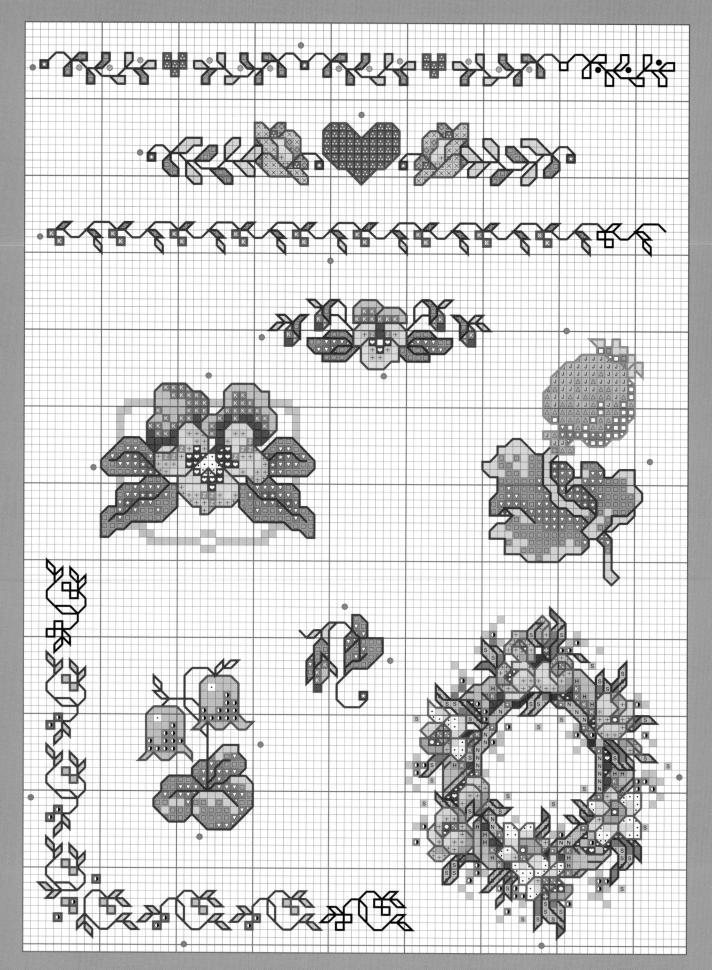

DMC Floss			
	XS	BS	FK
White	·		
745			
743	+		
741			
783	Z		
3825			
721	○		
720	E		
900	●	⌐	
353			
352	⊐		
351	U		
350			
606			
776	×		
899	◇		
309			
326		⌐	
211			
210	H		
209	K		
208			
327	♥	⌐	
827			
813	◑		
334			
825		⌐	
3811	J		
598	△		
597	□	⌐	
772			
3348	S		
3347			
3346	✚		
3345			
3364	▭		●
3363	▼		
3362	★		
890		⌐	
738	⊡		
437	N		
436	◪		
435	◨		
434			
920		⌐	●
801		⌐	
762			
318	▽		
414			
413	W	⌐	
310	▪	⌐	

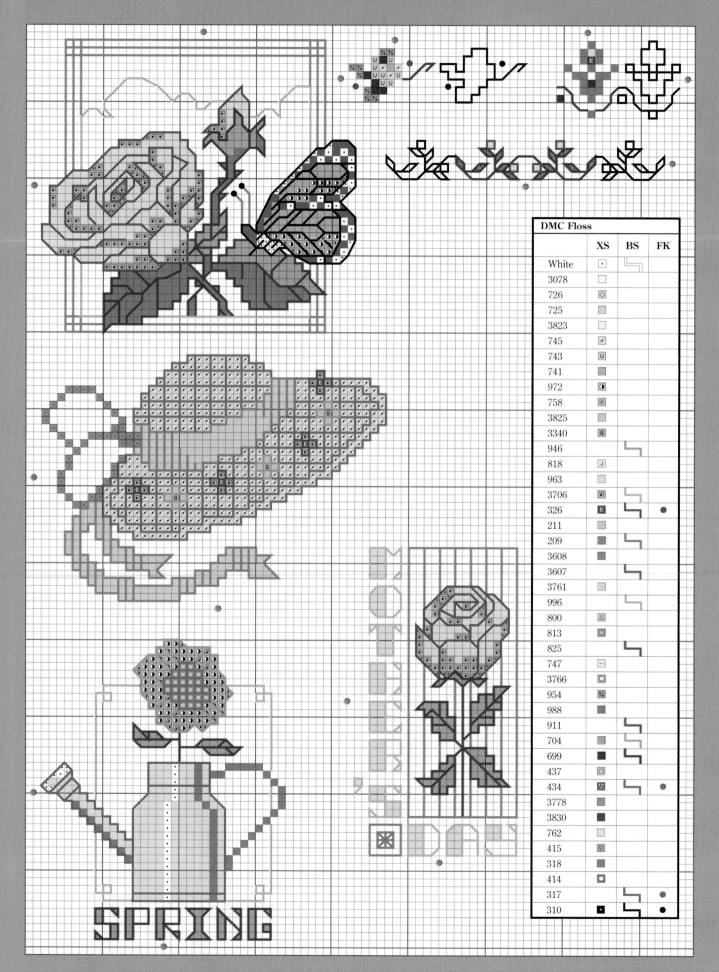

DMC Floss			
	XS	BS	FK
White	·		
3078			
726	◇		
725			
3823			
745	◪		
743	U		
741			
972	◑		
758	+		
3825			
3340	S		
946			
818	J		
963			
3706	▫		
326	E		●
211			
209	◉		
3608			
3607			
3761			
996			
800	△		
813	H		
825			
747	−		
3766	◎		
954	⊠		
988			
911			
704			
699	■		
437	▫		
434	▣		●
3778			
3830	▪		
762			
415	▽		
318			
414	▫		
317			●
310	▪		●

SPRING

SPRING PLANTING

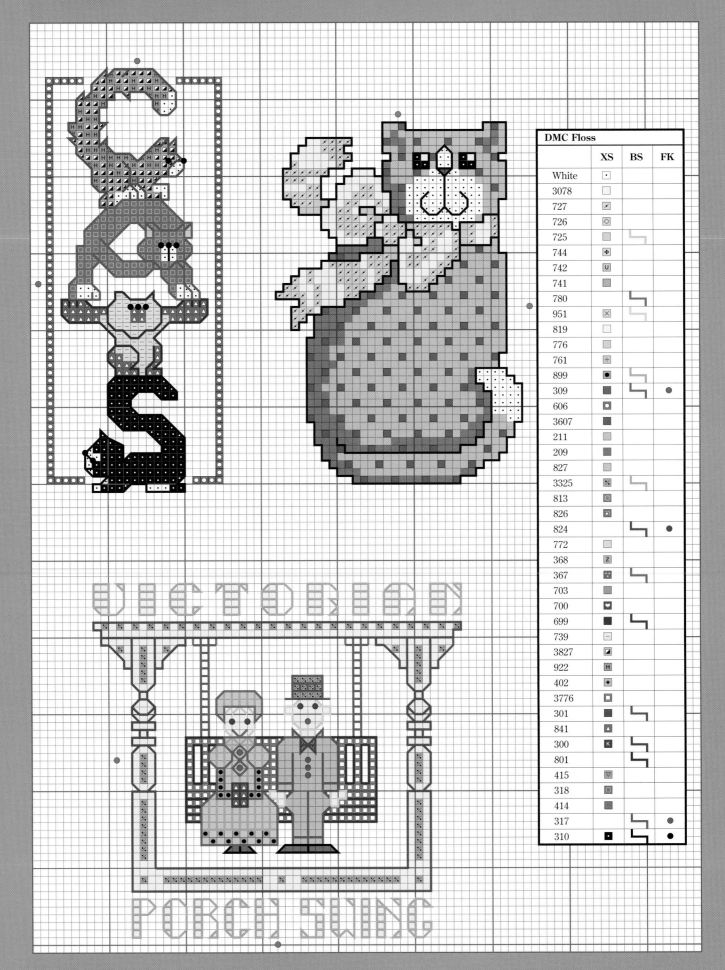

DMC Floss	XS	BS	FK
White	·		
3078			
727			
726			
725			
744	+		
742	U		
741			
780			
951	X		
819			
776			
761	+		
899	●		
309			●
606			
3607			
211			
209			
827			
3325			
813			
826			
824			●
772			
368	Z		
367			
703			
700			
699			
739	−		
3827			
922	H		
402	+		
3776			
301			
841	▲		
300	K		
801			
415	▽		
318			
414			
317			●
310	■		●

tulip

DMC Floss			
	XS	**BS**	**FK**
White	·		
3823			
727	⊠		
725			
744	Z		
742	△		
676	◖		
783			
780	⠶		
740	△		
721		⌐	
608	⅍		
606			
666	H		
963			
3716	⊟		
3806	U		
3805			
3804	★		
956	⊙		
321			
917	E	⌐	●
814		⌐	
554			
552	⊞		
550	■	⌐	
809			
813	◮		
826	◉		
824		⌐	
807	▣		
3813			
3816	K		
3815	▫		
702	▽		
3013			
3012	S		
3051		⌐	
3348			
989			
987	▼		
369	◪		
368			
320	◪		
319	■	⌐	
739	◇		
436	J		
3826	■	⌐	●
400	W		
801		⌐	
453	⁚		
452	♥		
451		⌐	
762			
318	▣		
317			
310	◼	⌐	●

Summer

Daze

Summer Daze Sampler   Top Left

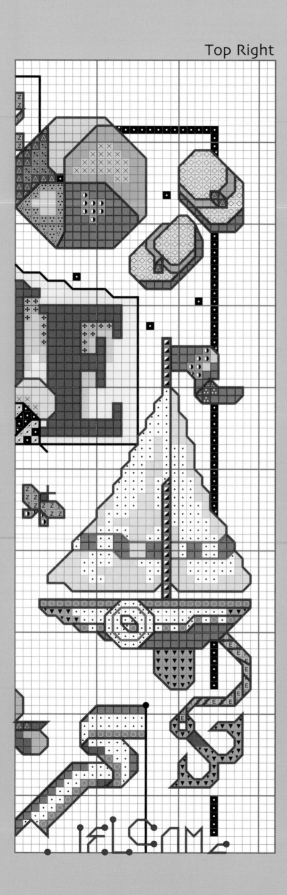

DMC Floss			
	XS	**BS**	**FK**
White	⊡		
746	☐		
745	◪		
744	☐		
743	U		
742	⊞		
741	◼		
754	☐		
722	H		
970	◑		
606	◼	⌐	●
776	∷		
899	Z	⌐	
321	▨		
3609	◻		
3608	▨		
3607	◼		
210	◻		
208	△		
*194	☐		
3761	⊠		
3755	◼	⌐	
826	◉		
797	◼	⌐	●
772	☐		
744 3348 }	⊞		
704	⁚⁚		
701	◼		
699	▲	⌐	
469	▣		
3770	◇		
3856	N		
402	E		
3776	◪		
920	★	⌐	
738	S		
842	◻		
841	▣		
839	◼	⌐	
762	☐		
415	▼		
413	◼	⌐	●
310	▣	⌐	●
*Kreinik fine braid			

Middle Center

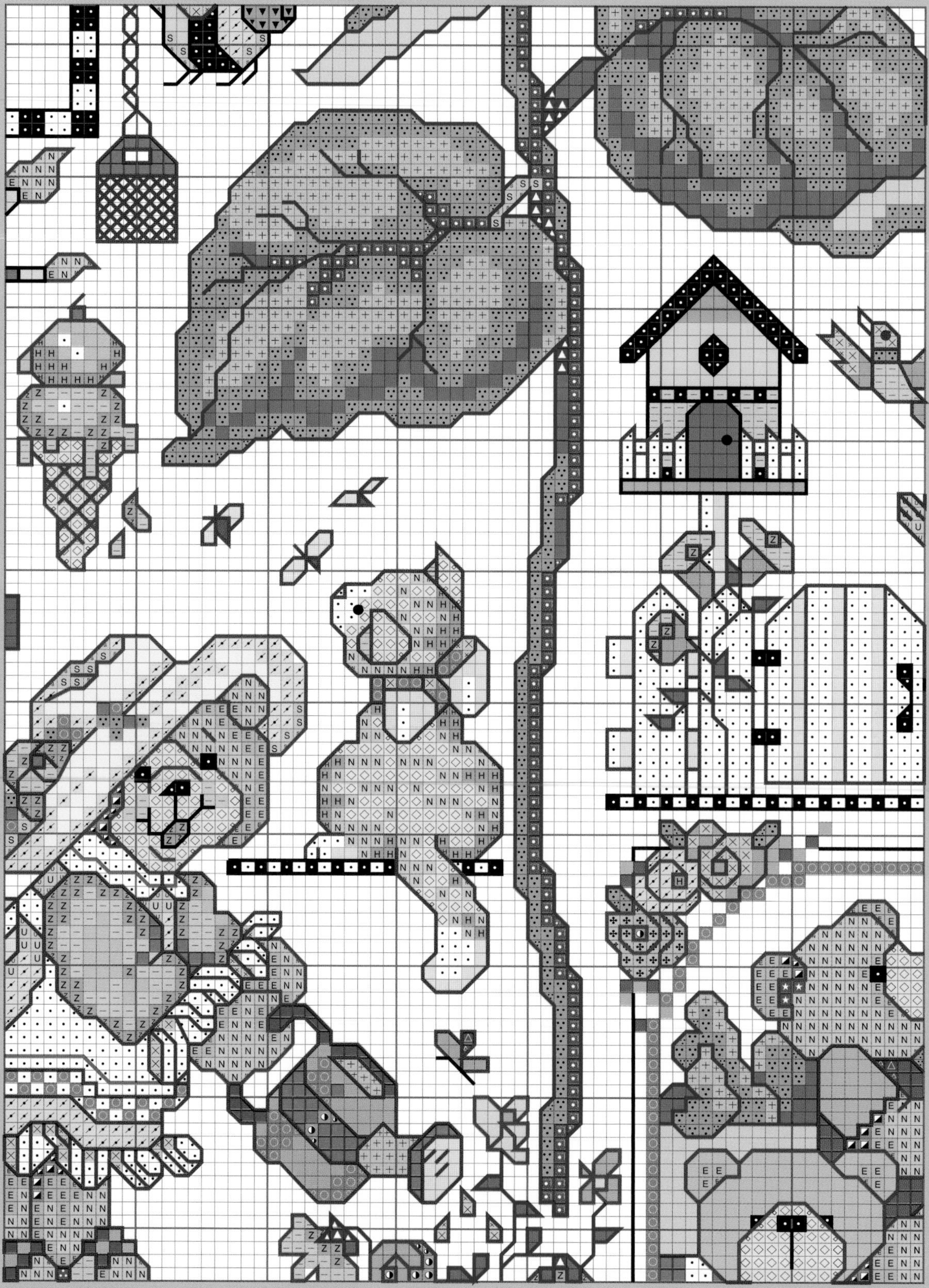

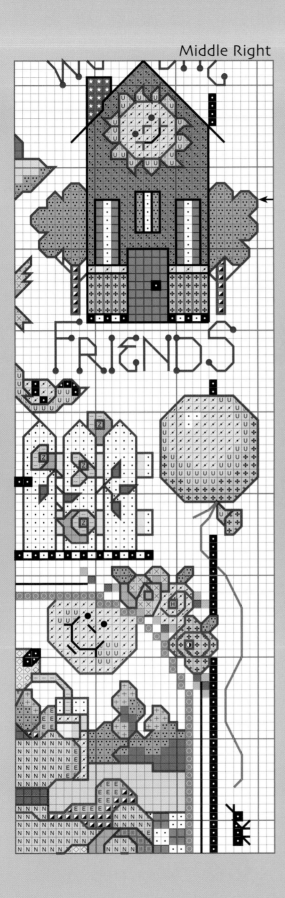

DMC Floss			
	XS	**BS**	**FK**
White	·		
746	▢		
745	◪		
744	▢		
743	U		
742	✚		
741	▣		
754	▢		
722	H		
970	◑		
606	▣	⌐	●
776	–		
899	Z	⌐	
321	⦂		
3609	▣		
3608	▨		
3607	▣		
210	▣		
208	△		
*194	▢		
3761	⊠		
3755	▣	⌐	
826	◉		
797	▣	⌐	●
772	▢		
744 3348 }	✚		
704	⦂		
701	▣		
699	▲	⌐	
469	▣		
3770	◇		
3856	N		
402	E		
3776	◪		
920	★	⌐	
738	S		
842	▣		
841	▣		
839	▣	⌐	
762	▢		
415	▼		
413	▣	⌐	●
310	▣	⌐	●
*Kreinik fine braid			

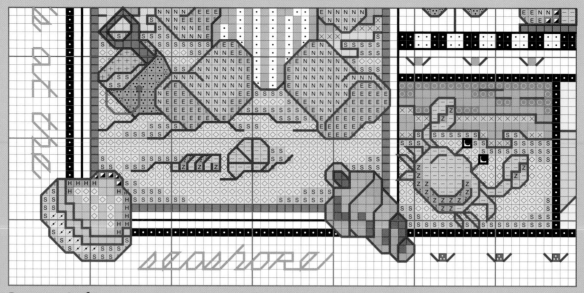

Bottom Left

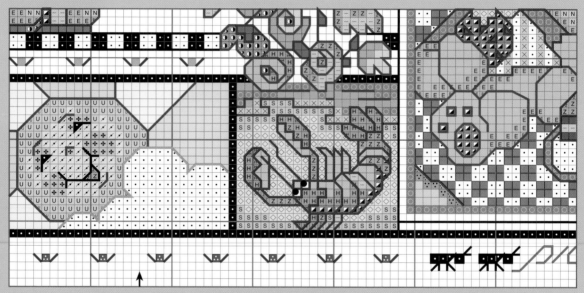

Bottom Center

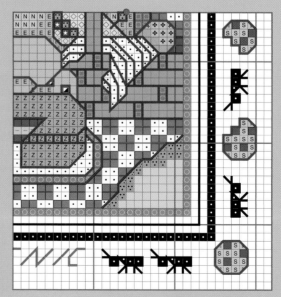

Bottom Right

DMC Floss			
	XS	BS	FK
White	·		
Ecru	⊠		
3823			
745			
744	U		
743			
741			
729	▲		
721			
761			
818			
3326	E		
335			
304	■	⌐	●
211			
209			
3837	■	⌐	
550			
800	+		
813			
826	★		
825		⌐	
747			
959	H		
3812	▽		
3813			
3816			
3815			
523			
3051	✚		
989	▲		
987			
319		⌐	
977	K		
3826	◉		
739	◇		
434	■		
754			
758	S		
3778			
950	J		
3773	◪		
3864			
3863	◎		
842	✦		
898	■	⌐	
413	■	⌐	
310	■	⌐	●

Say it
with
Flowers

Play

Croquet -

anyone?

TENNIS

Watch the Birdie

GONE FISHING

GOLF

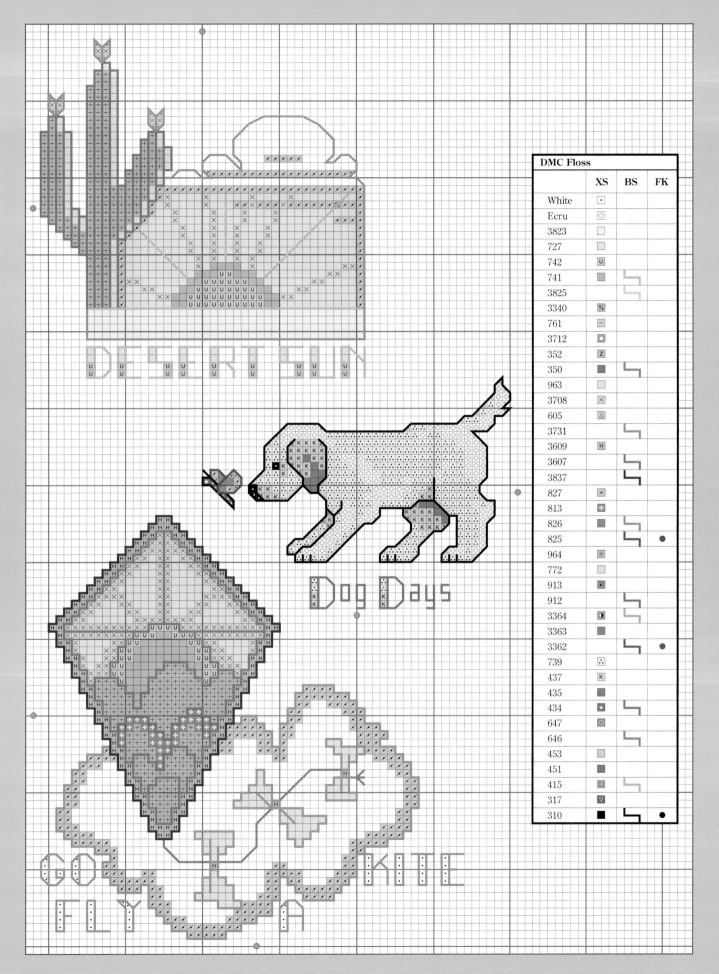

DESERT SUN

Dog Days

GO FLY A KITE

DMC Floss			
	XS	BS	FK
White	·		
Ecru	◇		
3823			
727			
742	U		
741		⌐	
3825			
3340			
761	-		
3712	◉		
352	Z		
350		⌐	
963			
3708	✕		
605	△		
3731		⌐	
3609	H		
3607		⌐	
3837		⌐	
827	⬈		
813	⊞		
826		⌐	
825		⌐	●
964	✚		
772			
913	⊡		
912		⌐	
3364	◑		
3363			
3362		⌐	●
739	⠒		
437	K		
435			
434	✦	⌐	
647	◎		
646		⌐	
453			
451			
415	▢	⌐	
317	▽		
310	■	⌐	●

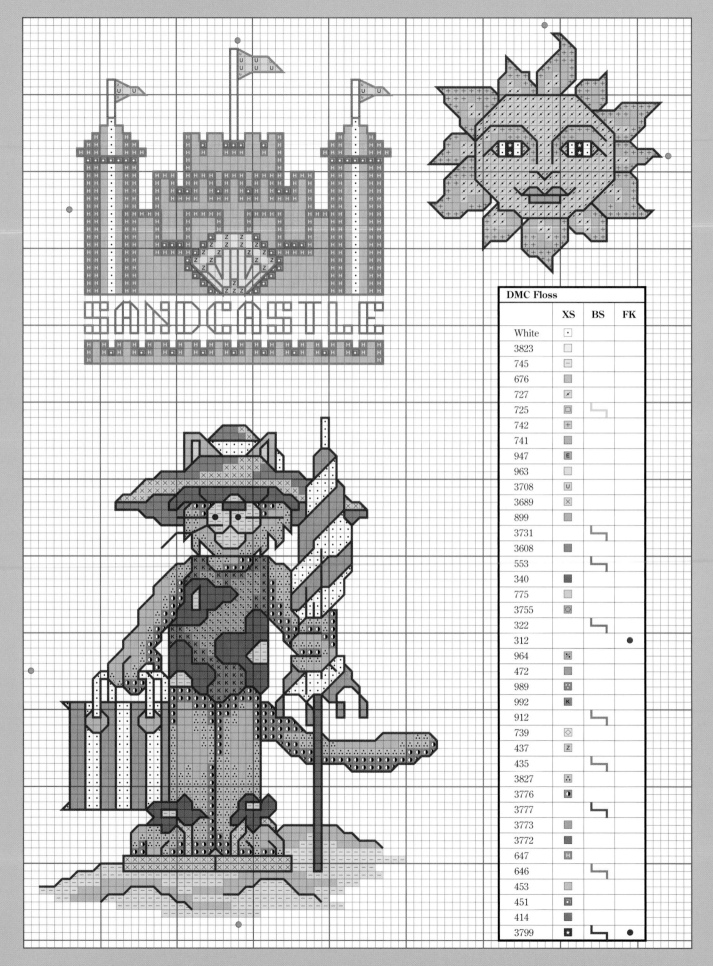

DMC Floss			
	XS	BS	FK
White	·		
3823			
745	−		
676			
727			
725	□	⌐	
742	+		
741			
947	E		
963			
3708	U		
3689	✕		
899			
3731		⌐	
3608			
553		⌐	
340			
775			
3755	◎		
322		⌐	
312			●
964	⅔		
472			
989	⊡		
992	K		
912		⌐	
739	◇		
437	Z		
435		⌐	
3827	⠿		
3776	◖		
3777		⌐	
3773			
3772			
647	H		
646		⌐	
453			
451	⊡		
414			
3799	✦	⌐	●

Summer is Cool

DMC Floss			
	XS	BS	FK
White	·		
3823	⊠		
727			
745	▽		
744	⟋		
743	▲		
741	K		
783	◻	⌐	
780	♥		
3824	▣		
3825	+		
3341	⦂		
3340	▨		
922	◐	⌐	
608	H		
606	◼	⌐	●
818	◻		
3326	J		
899	◎		
335	▲		
817	Z		
321	▫		
498	✚	⌐	●
211	▢		
209	⦂		
208	▨		
327		⌐	
799	▨		
798	⦂		
797	N	⌐	
772	▢		
3364	E		
3363	▨	⌐	●
3362		⌐	
989	◙		
987	⦂		
910	▽		
909	◼		
437	▬		
436	◿		
434	▨	⌐	
801		⌐	
762	▢		
415	U		
318	▢		
317	◼		
310	◼	⌐	●

Have a Berry

Nice Summer

Summer Thyme

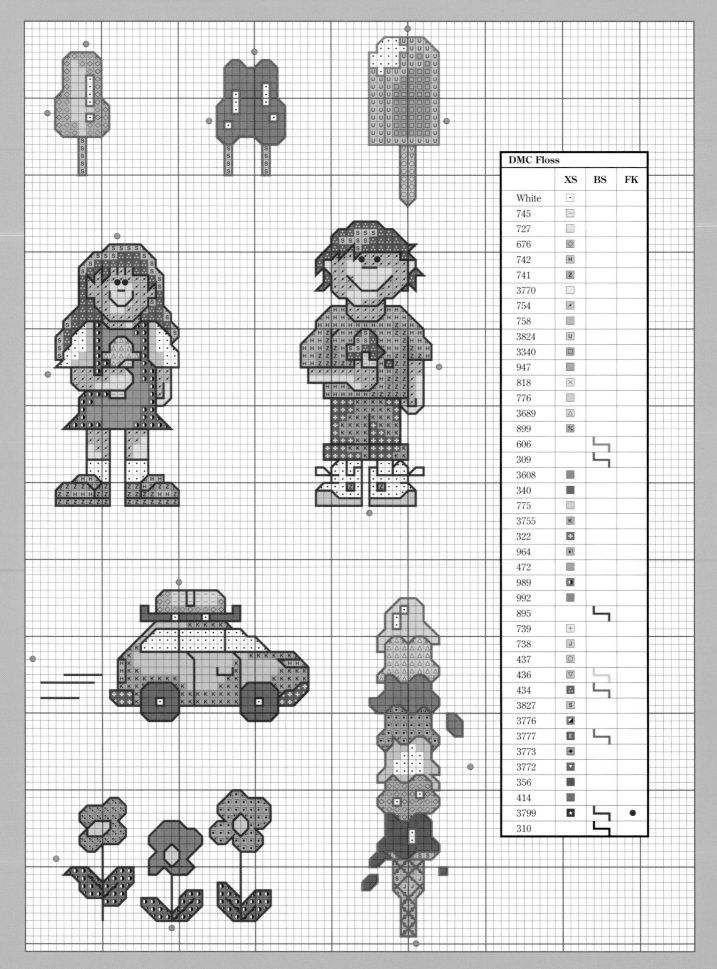

DMC Floss	XS	BS	FK
White	·		
745	−		
727	▦		
676	◈		
742	H		
741	Z		
3770	▢		
754	◪		
758	▦		
3824	U		
3340	▣		
947	▦		
818	✕		
776	▦		
3689	△		
899	▨		
606		⌐	
309		⌐	
3608	▪		
340	▪		
775	▦		
3755	K		
322	✦		
964	▪		
472	▦		
989	◑		
992	▪		
895		⌐	
739	+		
738	J		
437	○		
436	▽		
434	▦		
3827	S		
3776	◪		
3777	E		
3773	✦		
3772	▼		
356	▪		
414	▪		
3799	✪	⌐	●
310		⌐	

84

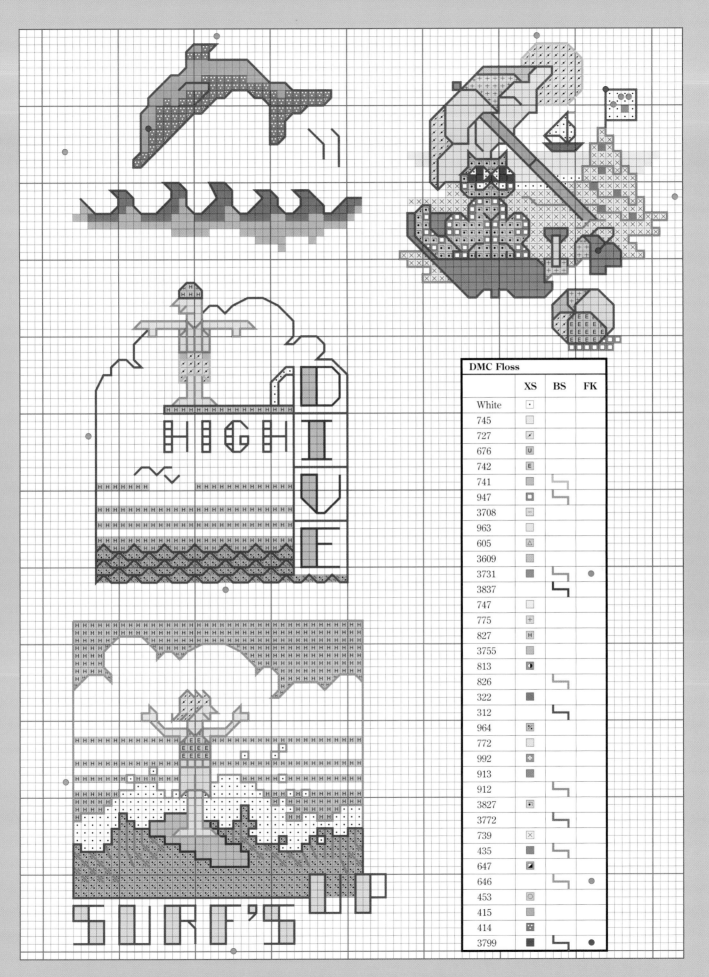

DMC Floss			
	XS	**BS**	**FK**
White	·		
745			
727			
676	U		
742	E		
741			
947			
3708	−		
963			
605	△		
3609			
3731			●
3837			
747			
775	+		
827	H		
3755			
813			
826			
322			
312			
964			
772			
992			
913			
912			
3827			
3772			
739	×		
435			
647			
646			●
453	○		
415			
414			
3799			●

DMC Floss			
	XS	BS	FK
White	·		
3823			
744			
742	+		
676	△		
783			
971	◐		
951	✕		
3825	◇		
722	E		
946	✚		
963			
3716	◎		
3806			
3326	▬		
335	▨		
891		⌐	
956	✚		
666	■		
349	▲		
304	▣	⌐	
211			
209			
552	▦		
550	■	⌐	
827			
3755	◑		
813	H		
826	◉		
824	■	⌐	
3813			
3816	U		
772			
704	◪		
702	■		
912	◢		
3348	▽		
989	K		
987	★		
986	■		
3013			
3052	▣		
3051	Z		
890	♥	⌐	
319	▨	⌐	
3779	J		
3778	▼		
3826	◻	⌐	
900		⌐	
842			
839		⌐	
415			
317		⌐	
310	▣	⌐	●

DMC Floss			
	XS	BS	FK
White	·		
712	⊗		
744	▣		
948	✕		
754	▣		
819	▢		
963	−		
776	◩		
899	▣		
666	▣		
335	U	⌐	
326			
498	K		
3609	▣		
3608	▨		
3607	▣		
718		⌐	
211	▣		
209	▲		
208	▣	⌐	
800	▣		
813	▽		
825		⌐	
809	N		
798	✛		
3761	⊡		
747	▢		
3766	E		
772	▢		
954	◑		
912	▣	⌐	
3052	▢		
739	Z		
435	▣		
3827	⊡		
402	◉		
301	✦		
400		⌐	
950	⊞		
3773	△		
3772	H	⌐	
840	▣		
839	▣		
838		⌐	
762	▢		
415	◪		
317	▣	⌐	
310	▣	⌐	●

DMC Floss			
	XS	BS	FK
White	·		
3823	☐		
745	↗		
744	☐		
676	Z		
742	✛		
783	■		
3824	–		
3340		⌐	
818	☐		
776	U		
605	✛		
3806	■		
3804	◎		
335		⌐	
3705	E		
666	■		
498	▣	⌐	
3609	◖		
3607	■	⌐	
915	✦		
211	☐		
209	▣		
552	▲		
550	K		
3756	☐		
775	△		
3325	H		
813	☐		
826	■	⌐	
747	✕		
3766	■		
806		⌐	
772	☐		
703	▣		
701	■		
955	☐		
954	◎		
911	✛	⌐	
3827	☐		
977	▽		
758	◎		
3773	■		
3778	◪		
355		⌐	
738	▣		
434		⌐	
762	☐		
415	▣		
317	■	⌐	
310	▣	⌐	●

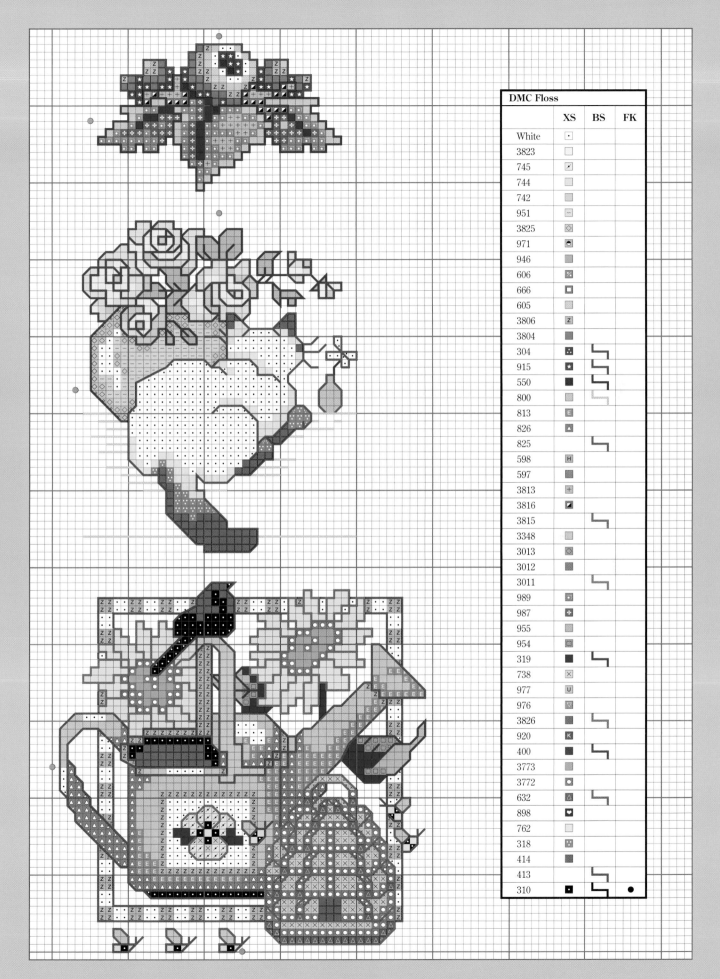

DMC Floss			
	XS	BS	FK
White	·		
3823			
745	⊿		
744			
742			
951	~		
3825	⬦		
971	◖		
946			
606	▨		
666	▫		
605			
3806	z		
3804			
304	▣	⌐	
915	★	⌐	
550	■	⌐	
800		⌐	
813	E		
826	▲		
825		⌐	
598	H		
597			
3813	+		
3816	◪		
3815		⌐	
3348			
3013	◎		
3012			
3011		⌐	
989	▣		
987	✚		
955			
954	▣		
319	■	⌐	
738	✕		
977	U		
976	▽		
3826		⌐	
920	K		
400	■	⌐	
3773			
3772	◒		
632	▲	⌐	
898	♥		
762			
318	▨		
414	■		
413		⌐	
310	◼	⌐	●

Autumn Harvest

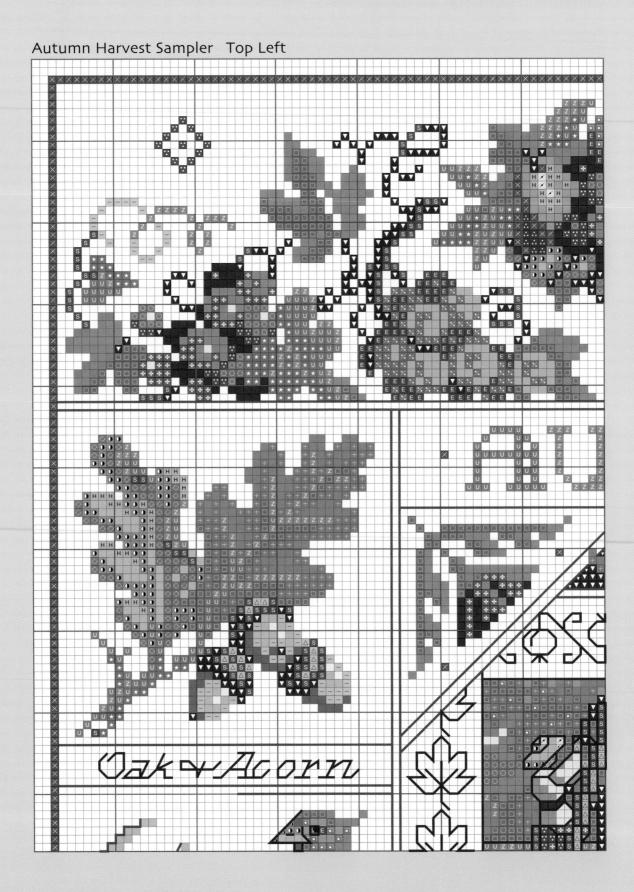

Oak & Acorn

Top Right

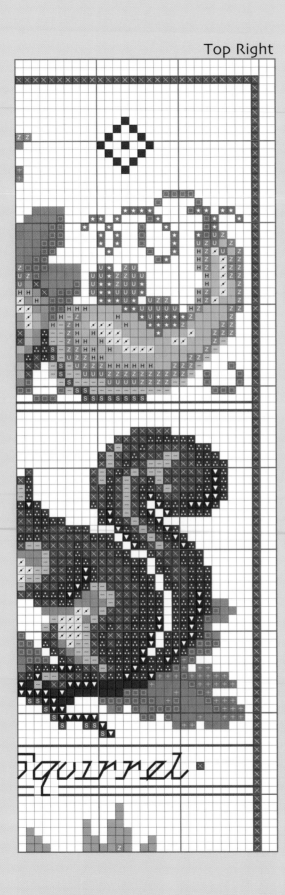

DMC Floss			
	XS	**BS**	**FK**
746	☐		
677	◪		
676	▣		
729	◕		
351 350 }	■		
350			●
3831	⊡		●
760 223 }	▣		
3722 3721 }	▨		
3802	E		
209	◎		
208	⊠		
341	▣		
340 3746 }	✚		
333	■	⌐	
471	▦		
988	⊞		
734	Z		
3012	U		
3011	★		
502	▣		
501 500 }	▣		
500		⌐	
436 435 }	▭		
435	◈	⌐	
434	■		
3854	H		
3853	▣		
301	⊠	⌐	
918	⊡		
3864	△		
3862	S		
898	▼	⌐	●
3371	■		
648	▣	⌐	

Pheasant

Apple tree

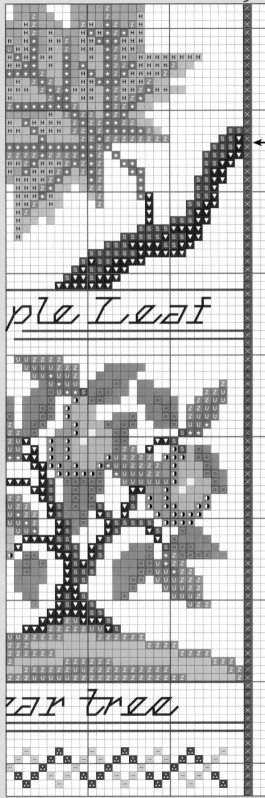

ple Leaf

ar tree

DMC Floss			
	XS	**BS**	**FK**
746	☐		
677	◩		
676	▦		
729	◖		
351 } 350	▦		
350			●
3831	▣		●
760 } 223	▦		
3722 } 3721	▨		
3802	E		
209	◉		
208	▦		
341	▦		
340 } 3746	✦		
333	■	⌐	
471	▦		
988	⊞		
734	Z		
3012	U		
3011	★		
502	▦		
501 } 500	▦		
500		⌐	
436 } 435	⊟		
435	◈	⌐	
434	▦		
3854	H		
3853	▦		
301	✕	⌐	
918	▦		
3864	△		
3862	S		
898	▼	⌐	●
3371	■		
648	▦	⌐	

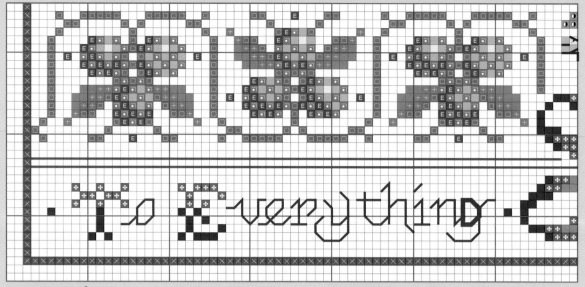

Bottom Left

Bottom Center

Bottom Right

DMC Floss		
	XS	BS
White	·	
3823	▢	
744	▢	
742	+	
971	▣	
3341	◪	
3340	◉	
946	◪	⌐
900	◼	⌐
608	▭	
606	▨	
666	H	
498	◷	⌐
3713	▢	
760	◈	
3806	▨	
3804	E	
915	◼	
813	▣	
826	▣	
825	✦	⌐
3807	▩	
792	◼	⌐
3813	▨	
3816	▨	⌐
3815		⌐
772	▢	
704	Z	
702	◼	
3348	⊠	
3347	▢	
3345	◼	
966	⌂	
955	U	
320	◨	
367	◬	
319	✚	⌐
3013	▨	
3012	N	
3052	♥	
3051	◼	⌐
3855	J	
3854	▨	
3827	▢	
976	◨	
975	K	⌐
3856	▽	
402	◑	
3830	◼	
355		⌐
762	▢	
3799	◼	⌐

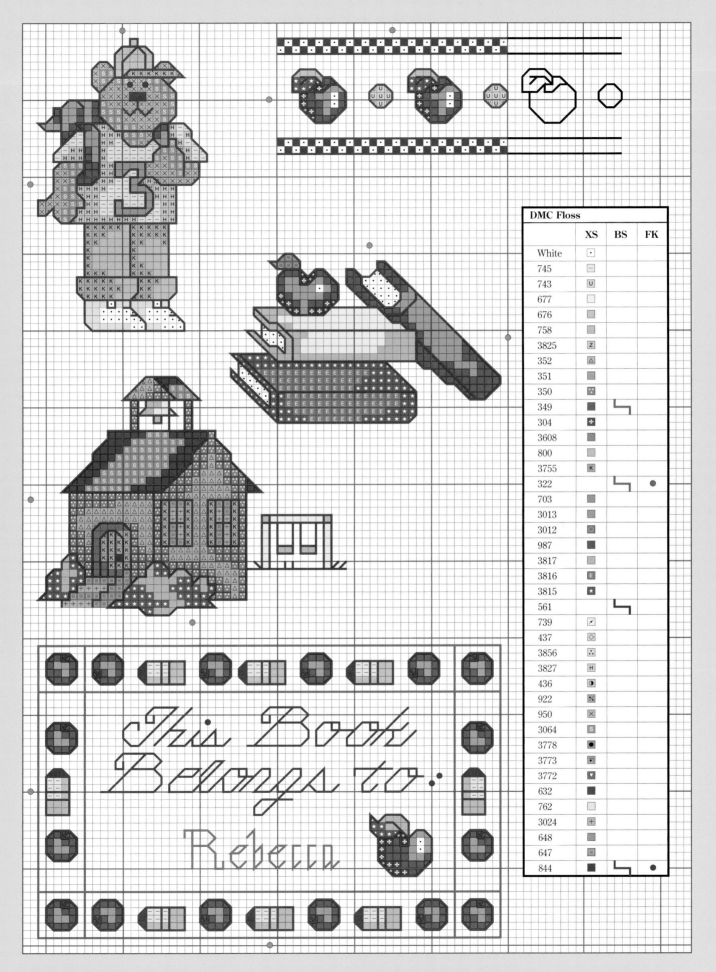

DMC Floss			
	XS	BS	FK
White	·		
745	−		
743	U		
677			
676			
758			
3825	Z		
352	△		
351			
350	⠿		
349		⌐	
304	✚		
3608			
800			
3755	K		
322		⌐	●
703			
3013			
3012	◎		
987			
3817			
3816	E		
3815	★	⌐	
561		⌐	
739	⟋		
437	◇		
3856	⠿		
3827	H		
436	◑		
922	⠿		
950	✕		
3064	S		
3778	●		
3773	⊡		
3772	▽		
632			
762			
3024	+		
648			
647	□		
844		⌐	●

DMC Floss			
	XS	**BS**	**FK**
White	·		
3823			
727			
725			
743	U		
783			
740	△		
3824			
608	+		
606		⌐	
761	Z		
760	◑		
818	⊠		
899	E		
309	⊠		
321	▣		
815	■	⌐	
772			
3348	▽		
907			
906	H		
905			
904		⌐	●
3364	▣		
3363	◎		
3362	■	⌐	
3856	–		
3827	J		
3854	N		
3853	▲		
739	⠰		
437	K		
435			
434		⌐	●
3779	◈		
3773	◪		
3772	✛		
841			
840	✦		
801		⌐	
415			
318	▫	⌐	
413	■	⌐	●

DMC Floss			
	XS	BS	FK
White	·		
712	J		
3823			
445			
744	◇		
743	◢		
677	△		
676	U		
783			
758	—		
971	Z		
722	▲		
946	◖	⌐	
819			
963	✕		
760		⌐	
351	✛		
349	⠶		●
816	■		
814	✚	⌐	●
3755			
322			
797		⌐	
772			
704			
988	⠶		
3013	K		
3012			
3011	□		
472	▽		
3345	⠶		
320	◪		
319	■	⌐	
945	S		
402	N		
3854	⅔		
739	✛		
3827	◎		
436	▼		
435	H	⌐	
921	◙		
3778	◗		
356	♥		
3863		⌐	
632	E		
400	★	⌐	●
762			
318	▣	⌐	
310	■	⌐	

DMC Floss			
	XS	BS	FK
White	·		
3823	▢		
744	▢		
742	+		
677	◿		
676	U		
783	▦		
948	▢		
3341	⊠		
722	◖		
353	⊟		
352	▦		
351	◺	⌐	
350	▦		
963	⊗		
899	H		
309	▦		
606	▣		
321	▽		
815		⌐	●
3325	▦		
334	◙		
322	▦	⌐	
3013	▦		
3012	▨		
3011	▦		
563	▦		
561	■	⌐	
739	Z		
436	E		
435	✚		
434	◘		
3855	∴		
3854	◪		
3826		⌐	
950	▦		
3773	N		
3064	◙		
3772	▦		
632	★		
801	◻	⌐	
3024	▽		
648	▦		
647	◺	⌐	
646			
844	■	⌐	●

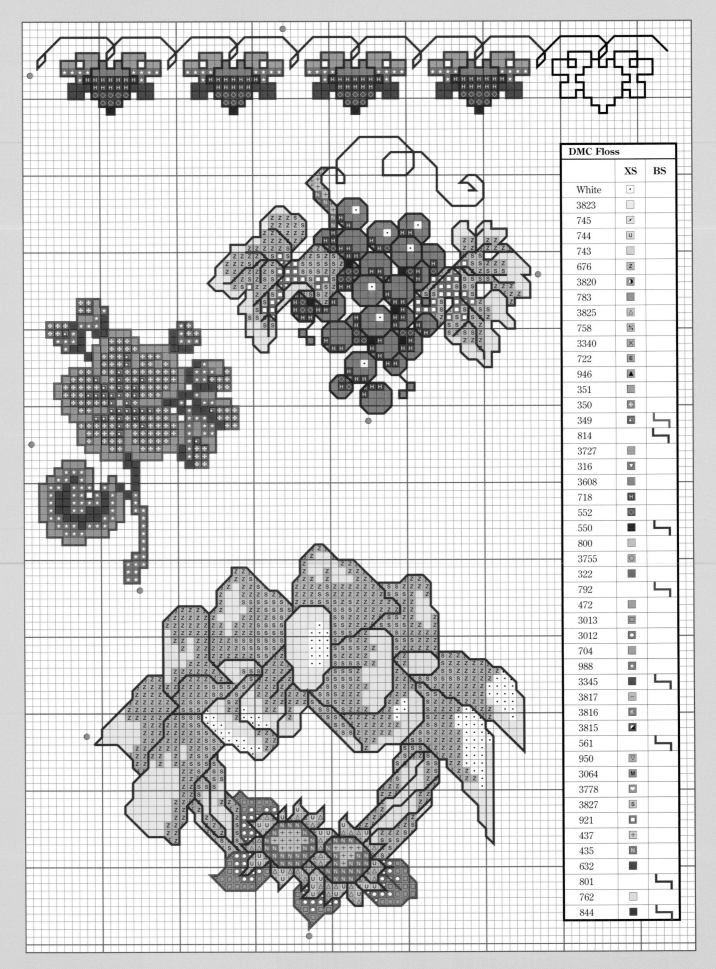

DMC Floss		
	XS	BS
White	·	
3823		
745		
744	U	
743		
676	Z	
3820		
783		
3825	△	
758	%	
3340	✕	
722	E	
946	▲	
351		
350		
349		⌐
814		⌐
3727		
316	▽	
3608		
718	H	
552	◇	
550	■	⌐
800		
3755	◎	
322		
792		⌐
472		
3013		
3012	◉	
704		
988		
3345	■	⌐
3817		
3816	K	
3815	◪	
561		⌐
950	▽	
3064	M	
3778		
3827	S	
921	□	
437	+	
435	N	
632	■	
801		⌐
762		
844	■	⌐

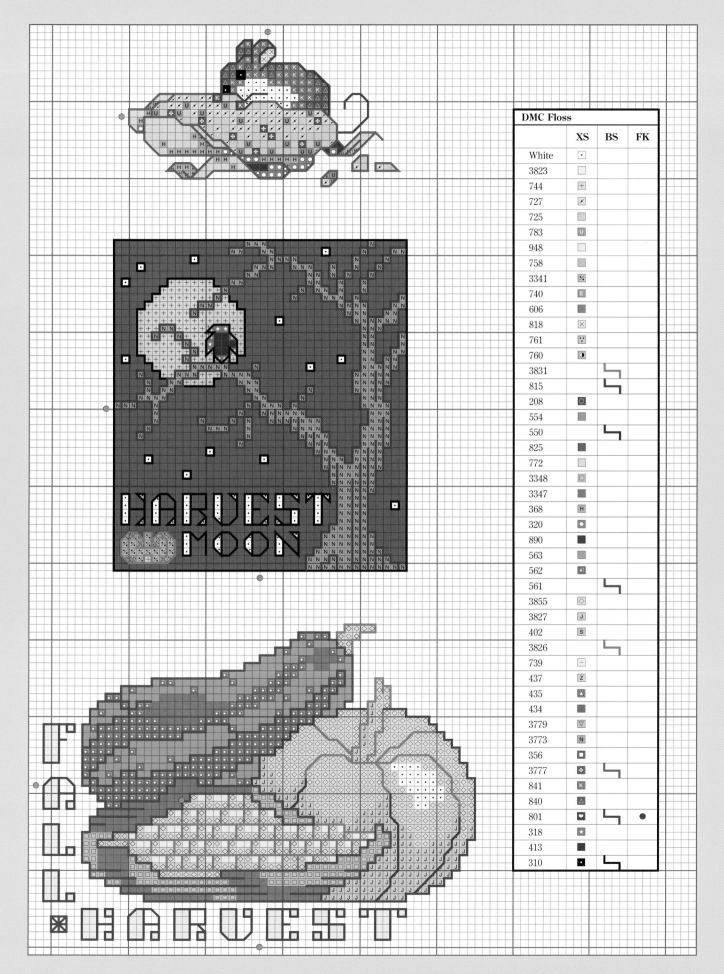

DMC Floss			
	XS	BS	FK
White	·		
3823			
744	+		
727			
725			
783	U		
948			
758			
3341			
740	E		
606			
818	X		
761			
760			
3831		⌐	
815		⌐	
208	O		
554			
550		⌐	
825			
772			
3348			
3347			
368	H		
320	O		
890			
563			
562			
561		⌐	
3855	◇		
3827	J		
402	S		
3826		⌐	
739	–		
437	Z		
435			
434			
3779	▽		
3773	N		
356			
3777			⌐
841	K		
840	△		
801	♥	⌐	●
318	★		
413			
310	■	⌐	

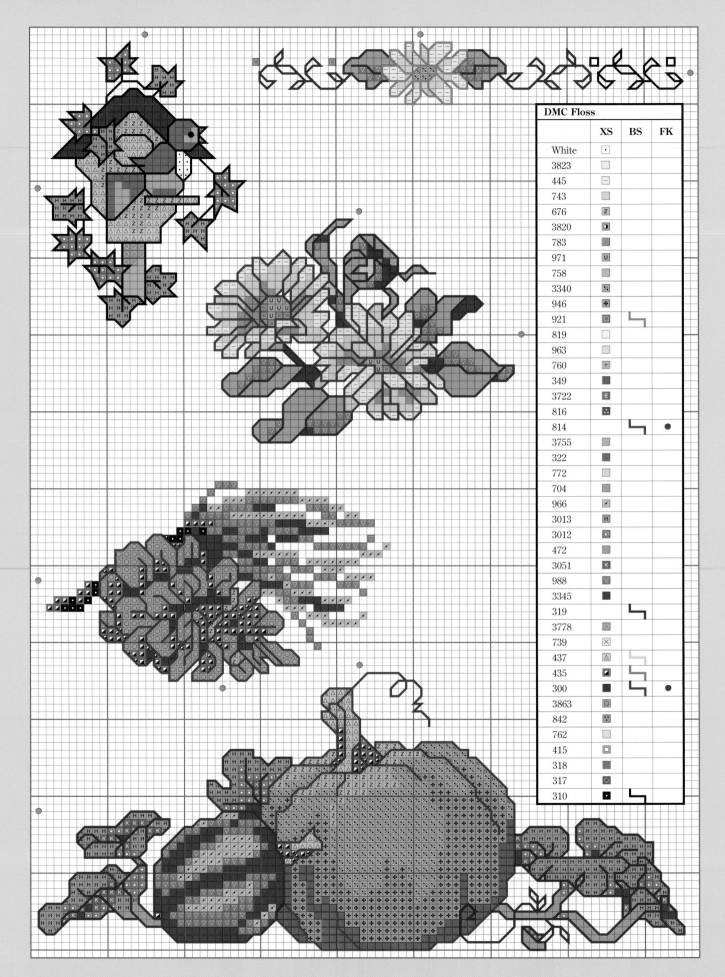

DMC Floss			
	XS	BS	FK
White	·		
3823			
445	−		
743			
676	Z		
3820	◐		
783			
971	U		
758			
3340	⅔		
946	✛		
921	▣	⌐	
819			
963			
760	+		
349	■		
3722	E		
816	▨		
814		⌐	●
3755			
322	▦		
772			
704			
966	◪		
3013	H		
3012	◘		
472			
3051	K		
988	▽		
3345	■		
319		⌐	
3778	◉		
739	⊠		
437	△	⌐	
435	◪	⌐	
300	■	⌐	●
3863	◎		
842	▨		
762			
415	◎		
318	▦		
317	◨		
310	■	⌐	

120

Have a Saucy
Season

DMC Floss			
	XS	BS	FK
White	⊡		○
3823	☐		
677	◪		
676			◉
745	◈		
744	☐		
754	⊞		
722	◼		
353	◧		
352	Ｚ		
349	◼	⌐	
3706	Ｈ		
3705	⊡		
606	✚		
3733	◑		
3609	Ｋ		
309	Ｅ		
210	◧		
209	△		
340	◼		
800	☐		
809	◎		
813	⊡		
826	★		
824		⌐	
959	▨		
958	◪		
3812	◼	⌐	
3013	◼		
3012	⊡		
3011	◕		
3051	◼		
935		⌐	
772	☐		
703	Ｕ		
701	◼		
699	♥		
989	▼		
987	Ｎ		
319	◼	⌐	
922	◙		
435	Ｓ		
3854	Ｊ		
3853	▼		
977	◙		
976	▨		
3826	▲	⌐	
356	▨		
407	◼		
632	☐		
402	⊟		
3776	Ｋ		
300	◼	⌐	
762	☐		
3799		⌐	●
310	◼	⌐	

DMC Floss			
	XS	BS	FK
White	·		
3823			
677			
676			
744	◇		
743	✕		
742	Z		
945	U		
3825			
353	J		
351	△		
350	★		
818			
3326	+		
956	H		
666	⊙		
498	■		
554			
553	I		
828			
827			
813	E		
825	■		
3013			
3011	■		
3052			
704	I		
702	♥		
966			
912	■		
320			
367	◘		
319			
3855	▽		
3854	S		
3853	◑		
739	−		
738			
301	☐		
3774	N		
950	+		
3773			
407	◪		
3772	+		
841			
839	■		
453			
452	△		
451	K		
318			
3799	■		
310	■		●

Anchor Conversion Chart

DMC	Anchor	DMC	Anchor	DMC	Anchor	DMC	Anchor	DMC	Anchor
B5200	1	371	887	580	924	734	279	824	164
White	2	372	887	581	281	738	361	825	162
Ecru	387	400	351	597	1064	739	366	826	161
208	110	402	1047	598	1062	740	316	827	160
209	109	407	914	600	59	741	304	828	9159
210	108	413	236	601	63	742	303	829	906
211	342	414	235	602	57	743	302	830	277
221	897	415	398	603	62	744	301	831	277
223	895	420	374	604	55	745	300	832	907
224	893	422	372	605	1094	746	275	833	874
225	1026	433	358	606	334	747	158	834	874
300	352	434	310	608	330	754	1012	838	1088
301	1049	435	365	610	889	758	9575	839	1086
304	19	436	363	611	898	760	1022	840	1084
307	289	437	362	612	832	761	1021	841	1082
309	42	444	291	613	831	762	234	842	1080
310	403	445	288	632	936	772	259	844	1041
311	148	451	233	640	393	775	128	869	375
312	979	452	232	642	392	776	24	890	218
315	1019	453	231	644	391	778	968	891	35
316	1017	469	267	645	273	780	309	892	33
317	400	470	266	646	8581	781	308	893	27
318	235	471	265	647	1040	782	308	894	26
319	1044	472	253	648	900	783	307	895	1044
320	215	498	1005	666	46	791	178	898	380
321	47	500	683	676	891	792	941	899	38
322	978	501	878	677	361	793	176	900	333
326	59	502	877	680	901	794	175	902	897
327	101	503	876	699	923	796	133	904	258
333	119	504	206	700	228	797	132	905	257
334	977	517	162	701	227	798	146	906	256
335	40	518	1039	702	226	799	145	907	255
336	150	519	1038	703	238	800	144	909	923
340	118	520	862	704	256	801	359	910	230
341	117	522	860	712	926	806	169	911	205
347	1025	523	859	718	88	807	168	912	209
349	13	524	858	720	325	809	130	913	204
350	11	535	401	721	324	813	161	915	1029
351	10	543	933	722	323	814	45	917	89
352	9	550	101	725	305	815	44	918	341
353	8	552	99	726	295	816	43	919	340
355	1014	553	98	727	293	817	13	920	1004
356	1013	554	95	729	890	818	23	921	1003
367	216	561	212	730	845	819	271	922	1003
368	214	562	210	731	281	820	134	924	851
369	1043	563	208	732	281	822	390	926	850
370	888	564	206	733	280	823	152	927	849

DMC	Anchor	DMC	Anchor	DMC	Anchor	DMC	Anchor	DMC	Anchor
928	274	3021	905	3722	1027	3816	876	114	1213
930	1035	3022	8581	3726	1018	3817	875	115	1206
931	1034	3023	899	3727	1016	3818	923	121	1210
932	1033	3024	388	3731	76	3819	278	122	1215
934	862	3031	905	3733	75	3820	306	123	——
935	861	3032	898	3740	872	3821	305	124	1210
936	846	3033	387	3743	869	3822	295	125	1213
937	268	3041	871	3746	1030	3823	386	126	1209
938	381	3042	870	3747	120	3824	8		
939	152	3045	888	3750	1036	3825	323		
943	189	3046	887	3752	1032	3826	1049		
945	881	3047	852	3753	1031	3827	311		
946	332	3051	845	3755	140	3828	373		
947	330	3052	844	3756	1037	3829	901		
948	1011	3053	843	3760	162	3830	5975		
950	4146	3064	883	3761	928				
951	1010	3072	397	3765	170	Variegated			
954	203	3078	292	3766	167	Colors			
955	203	3325	129	3768	779				
956	40	3326	36	3770	1009	48	1207		
957	50	3328	1024	3772	1007	51	1220		
958	187	3340	329	3773	1008	52	1209		
959	186	3341	328	3774	778	53	——		
961	76	3345	268	3776	1048	57	1203		
962	75	3346	267	3777	1015	61	1218		
963	23	3347	266	3778	1013	62	1201		
964	185	3348	264	3779	868	67	1212		
966	240	3350	77	3781	1050	69	1218		
970	925	3354	74	3782	388	75	1206		
971	316	3362	263	3787	904	90	1217		
972	298	3363	262	3790	904	91	1211		
973	290	3364	261	3799	236	92	1215		
975	357	3371	382	3801	1098	93	1210		
976	1001	3607	87	3802	1019	94	1216		
977	1002	3608	86	3803	69	95	1209		
986	246	3609	85	3804	63	99	1204		
987	244	3685	1028	3805	62	101	1213		
988	243	3687	68	3806	62	102	1209		
989	242	3688	75	3807	122	103	1210		
991	1076	3689	49	3808	1068	104	1217		
992	1072	3705	35	3809	1066	105	1218		
993	1070	3706	33	3810	1066	106	1203		
995	410	3708	31	3811	1060	107	1203		
996	433	3712	1023	3812	188	108	1220		
3011	856	3713	1020	3813	875	111	1218		
3012	855	3716	25	3814	1074	112	1201		
3013	853	3721	896	3815	877	113	1210		

Metric Equivalancy Chart

mm-millimetres cm-centimetres
inches to millimetres and centimetres

inches	mm	cm	inches	cm	inches	cm
⅛	3	0.3	9	22.9	30	76.2
¼	6	0.6	10	25.4	31	78.7
⅜	10	1.0	11	27.9	32	81.3
½	13	1.3	12	30.5	33	83.8
⅝	16	1.6	13	33.0	34	86.4
¾	19	1.9	14	35.6	35	88.9
⅞	22	2.2	15	38.1	36	91.4
1	25	2.5	16	40.6	37	94.0
1¼	32	3.2	17	43.2	38	96.5
1½	38	3.8	18	45.7	39	99.1
1¾	44	4.4	19	48.3	40	101.6
2	51	5.1	20	50.8	41	104.1
2½	64	6.4	21	53.3	42	106.7
3	76	7.6	22	55.9	43	109.2
3½	89	8.9	23	58.4	44	111.8
4	102	10.2	24	61.0	45	114.3
4½	114	11.4	25	63.5	46	116.8
5	127	12.7	26	66.0	47	119.4
6	152	15.2	27	68.6	48	121.9
7	178	17.8	28	71.1	49	124.5
8	203	20.3	29	73.7	50	127.0

Index